Titus

Living a **CHRIST-CENTERED** Life
in a **SELF-CENTERED** World

A Six-week Bible Study by
Rand Hummel

Other Titles by Rand Hummel

Colossians: Jesus Christ—The Visible Icon of the Invisible God
The Dark Side of the Internet
Fear Not
Five Smooth Stones
God & I Time Treasures Volume 1 & 2
God is...Learning About My God
James: A Guidebook to Spiritual Maturity
Jonah's Magnificent God
Joseph: A Man With Character
Lest You Fall
New Testament Postcards
I Peter: Living in the Face of Ridicule
Philippians—The Secret of Outrageous, Contagious Joy!
Turn Away Wrath
What Does God Say About My Sin?

All Scripture is quoted from the Authorized King James Version.

Titus: Living a Christ-Centered Life in a Self-Centered World
Third Edition
A Six-week Bible Study
By Rand Hummel
Cover design by Craig Stouffer

© 2009, 2005, 2003 THE WILDS Christian Association, Inc.
PO Box 509
Taylors, SC 29687
Phone: (864) 268-4760
Fax: (864) 292-0743

ISBN: 978-0-9815235-7-6

TITUS
Living a CHRIST-CENTERED Life in a SELF-CENTERED World

Week 1: Watch Out for Self-Centeredness! Titus 1:1-9

Week 2: Watch Out for Stubbornness! Titus 1:10-16

Week 3: Watch Out for Slothfulness! Titus 2:1-8

Week 4: Watch Out for Sinfulness! Titus 2:9-15

Week 5: Watch Out for Spiritual Amnesia! Titus 3:1-8

Week 6: Watch Out for Selfishness! Titus 3:9-15

DEAR READERS,

The world has a way of creeping into our lives. It is not easy to live a Christ-centered life in our self-centered world. Our personal stubbornness, slothfulness, sinfulness, and selfishness are evidence to the world's constant influence on our lives.

For the next six weeks, as you study Paul's inspired advice to Titus, you will see that the transformation that Christ makes in salvation, the enablement Christ gives through His grace, and the hope of Christ's imminent return will help us to keep our focus on our Lord Jesus Christ and off self.

Titus was one of those guys you just loved to be around, but he had a difficult task reaching out to the self-centered islanders of Crete. His Christ-centered teaching, God-focused ministry, and Spirit-filled living impacted the Cretians for eternity. God can do the same through your life as you follow the example Titus left for us.

Sincerely yours,

Rand Hummel

My Dear Son Titus,

To effectively evangelize and reach the island of Crete through the young church that has been started, you must understand what and who you are facing. You will find four kinds of people. Some are hopelessly depending on their own works for eternal life. You will meet those whose mission in life is to argue with everything you teach. Others have left the argumentative stage and are actually teaching lies and confusing young believers. There are also many young spiritual leaders who must be encouraged to mature in such a way that their lives are free from hypocrisy or accusations of selfishness and wickedness. Titus, you have your hands full, but remember that you are simply sharing with these Cretians what I have shared with you...Jesus Christ. He is the Truth for those spreading lies and false teaching. He is the Answer to all those questions others want to argue about. He is the Example for all believers to follow. Take what you know about your God and Saviour, Jesus Christ, and allow Him to use you to capture the island of Crete.

Sincerely yours for Cretians,

Paul

Monday
AS A LEADER, PAUL ATTACKS SELF-CENTEREDNESS.
Titus 1:1-4

....

Paul, a servant of God, and an apostle of Jesus Christ, according to the faith of God's elect, and the acknowledging of the truth which is after godliness; In hope of eternal life, which God, that cannot lie, promised before the world began; But hath in due times manifested His Word through preaching, which is committed unto me according to the commandment of God our Saviour; To Titus, mine own son after the common faith: Grace, mercy, and peace, from God the Father and the Lord Jesus Christ our Saviour.

....

1. Most little kids have played the game "Follow the Leader" by skipping, jumping, spinning, crawling, or running around a playground imitating what the leader does. Paul encourages us to also "Follow the Leader." The first four verses of Titus 1 explain the Apostle Paul's personal attack on a self-centered lifestyle. There are at least five principles Paul emphasizes in these verses that reveal how the apostle refused to focus on himself and instead focused on God and others. Answer the questions below from Titus 1:1-4.

Paul was a **servant**, a slave, not for himself, but to whom? _____

Paul was an **apostle**, an ambassador, not for himself, but of whom?_____

Paul was a **preacher**, not by his choosing, but by whose command? _____

Paul was **committed** to helping what young preacher? _____

2. Paul was a balanced theologian speaking of **faith** and **election** in the same breath. There are some mysteries in God's Word that have been argued and discussed for hundreds of years without total agreement from godly men on both sides of the issues. We should never become so spiritually arrogant that we think we totally understand the mind of God. God works in our hearts as He draws us to Himself at which time we must put our faith and trust in Him. That is salvation! Briefly write out your personal testimony when you were called of God and put your trust in Him for **eternal** salvation. _____

_____

3. The greatest enemy of a self-centered, selfish life is a strong focus on God and others. As a slave and an ambassador, Paul was called of God to serve those whom God called to salvation. Another way of saying **acknowledging of the truth which is after godliness** is *to help people understand God's truth in a way that leads to godliness.* How would you define *godliness*?_____

_____

_____

4. **Godliness** is *more than simply being godlike; it is actually a way of thinking.* **Godliness** is a CHRIST-CENTERED mentality unlike the postmodernistic, selfish, self-centered thinking of today's society. **Godliness** is a result of three things: a dependence on God, a devotion to God, and a desire for God. On a scale from 1 to 10, with 1 being low and 10 being high, rate yourself on how you/your:

_____ *Depend on God* for wisdom and strength on a daily basis.
_____ *Devotion to God* through serving and worship.
_____ *Desire for God* by your consistency in Bible study and prayer.

According to the way you just rated yourself, would you consider yourself a *godly* Christian? _____

5. Read verse 2. The **hope** mentioned in this verse is not an "I hope so" type of hope, but actually a *confident expectation* that it will happen. What does this verse say **God promised before the world began**? _____

Since God will always keep His promises and will never lie to us, how long does **eternal life** last?

_____

What phrase does John 3:16 use to describe **eternal life**? _____

How could God's promise of everlasting and **eternal life** help you when you begin to doubt your salvation? _____

_____

6. According to verse 3, how does God communicate His **truth** to people today? _____

_____

How many times do you hear Bible **preaching** each week? _____

Who are some of your favorite preachers? _____

_____

What makes a "good" preacher? _____

_____

List three practical ways to get the most out of a message preached. I'll help you with the first one:

• Take notes

• _____

• _____

For you guys, have you ever considered surrendering your life to God to preach as a pastor, missionary, or evangelist? _____

7. How did Paul describe **Titus** in verse 4? _____

_____

When Paul called **Titus** his **own** _son_, he meant that _he personally introduced him to Jesus Christ._ Is there anyone you have been responsible for leading to the Lord?_____

What is their name?_____

You may say, "Well, I don't have what it takes to be a soulwinner; I'm just a sower." No problem! Have you "adopted" a son who has already been saved in order to help him grow and mature? _____

What do you do each week that helps someone grow closer to the Lord? _____

_____

According to Titus 1:1-4, how did Paul personally attack self-centeredness?

Tuesday
Leaders need to be blameless (not self-centered)
IN THEIR FAMILY LIFE.
Titus 1:5-6

For this cause left I thee in Crete, that thou shouldest set in order the things that are wanting, and ordain elders in every city, as I had appointed thee: If any be blameless, the husband of one wife, having faithful children not accused of riot or unruly.

1. **Crete**, now called Candia, is an island only 158 miles long off the coast of Italy. For what two reasons was Titus left on the island of **Crete**? _____

_____

Titus was called to serve the people of **Crete** who were known as a self-centered lot. This island was inhabited by mercenary soldiers, traders, and pirates who lived for self and self alone. Describe the type of friends God has called you to serve. _____

_____

_____

2. Paul encouraged Titus to **set in order the things that are wanting**. The phrase **set in order** is from the Greek word *orthos* where we get our word orthodontist, a dental specialist who straightens crooked teeth. Have you ever had braces? (I used to love watching the dentist spread my kid's lips wide open with that weird contraption to get to their teeth.) Some of Crete's leaders were crooked and way out of line. They needed straightening out. Match the following verses with the areas of life that Titus emphasized to the leaders.

Titus 1:6	Blameless in their preaching ministries
Titus 1:7	Blameless in their public lives
Titus 1:8	Blameless in their personal lives
Titus 1:9	Blameless in their family lives

3. From Titus 1:5, what was Titus' second job?_____

There were so many sorry teachers and leaders in the church of Crete, Paul wanted Titus **to ordain elders** or leaders in each city who would teach God's truth. If your church had more spiritual leaders rather than worldly leaders, how would that change the peer pressure and spiritual temperature of your church?

_____

_____

If we have more good leaders than bad leaders, we will have more good churches than bad churches. How could God use you personally to encourage spiritual leaders to take a stand for God and against selfishness in your church?_____

_____

4. The word **blameless** means *above reproach, not-chargeable, without blame, unquestioned integrity, and unimpeachable*. It does not mean sinless perfection! It does mean that the spiritual leaders in our churches should have a great testimony! Everyone of us should seek to have a **blameless** testimony. In Titus 1:6 Paul told Titus to ordain leaders who were **husbands** of how many wives? _____
Actually, the phrase **husband of one wife** means a *one-woman man*. Girls, from the explanations on the next page, describe the kind of **blameless** guy you would want for a husband; or guys, describe the kind

of **blameless husband** you want to be. _____

_____

A one-woman man is a man who is devoted to the one woman who is his wife.

A one-woman man keeps his heart and his eyes focused on her.

A one-woman man does not just avoid divorce, he advocates faithfulness.

A one-woman man guards himself against strange women who slay strong men.

5. According to Titus 1:6, Titus was looking for mature leaders who loved their wives and had what kind of kids? _____

Having faithful children actually means *a man whose children believe.* If a man's children reject the Truth of the Gospel, even though he may have the desire and talents for a spiritual leader, his **children** disqualify him. A good leader's **children** cannot be accused of being **unruly** or **riotous**. Circle the six phrases below that refer to **unruly** and underline the four that mean **riotous.**

not willing to submit	wasteful	undisciplined	pleasure seeking
unsubmissive	excessive spender	disobedient	refusal to be ruled by others
	party mentality	children who are their own boss	

Write out 3 John 4._____

_____

Explain in your own words how a man's children could disqualify him from the preaching ministry of a local church. _____

_____

If your dad was a pastor, missionary, or evangelist, is there anything in your life that would disqualify him from the ministry? _____

If there is, you need to get with God and your parents to make those things right.

6. In Titus 1:5 Paul used the phrase **the things that are wanting**. This phrase refers to *the things that are lacking in spiritual leaders' lives.*

Write out Psalm 23:1. _____

_____

To **want** is *to lack, to need, or to be without.* What area of your Christian life is empty, **wanting**, lacking, or in need? _____

How can God fill that need or want?_____

_____

According to Titus 1:5-6, how can leaders be blameless
and not self-centered in their family life?

11

Wednesday

LEADERS NEED TO BE BLAMELESS (NOT SELF-CENTERED) IN THEIR PERSONAL LIFE.
Titus 1:7

For a bishop must be blameless, as the steward of God; not selfwilled, not soon angry, not given to wine, no striker, not given to filthy lucre.

1. There are three words describing the spiritual leaders Titus worked with in Crete. The first is **elder** which refers to *the person*, the second is **bishop** which refers to *the office of an overseer,* and the third is **steward** which refers to *the leader's duties*; all refer to the same person. What is the one major characteristic of a **steward** according to 1 Corinthians 4:2? _____

What does Hebrews 13:17 and 1 Thessalonians 5:12-14 teach us about how we are supposed to treat the spiritual leaders over us? _____

_____

2. It is interesting that the word **blameless** is repeated in verses 6 and 7 which obviously shows that Paul wanted to emphasize this character trait. **Blameless** means *to be above reproach, unaccused, or not-chargeable.* The **blameless** leader would not be accused of selfish conduct. Have you ever been "called in" to the boss's office? _____

Some, even if they did not do anything wrong, have a reputation of getting into trouble and are the first ones to be accused when there is a problem. Have you ever thought or said something like, "Why is everyone looking at me?" or "Why are they blaming me? I didn't do anything!" We are known for our extremes. What do most people know or think about you? _____

_____

3. Titus 1:7 describes the character of a **blameless** man by listing five negatives first. These negatives relate to five areas of extreme temptation, namely pride, **anger**, alcohol, power, and money. Constant exposure to these things is an occupational hazard for all Christian leaders. All five challenge us to self-mastery and self-control. Write out the four "nots" and the one "no" of the leader below, and we will study them in detail.

• not _____

• not _____

• not _____

• no_____

• not _____

4. **Not selfwilled**: The Greek words for **selfwilled** literally mean *to please self.* Someone has said that he who falls in love with himself will have no rivals. Do you know anyone who is so self-centered that they pout or pitch a fit if they do not get their own way?_____

What areas of self-will do you struggle with the most? _____

_____

5. **Not soon angry**: **Angry** people do not make good leaders. There are two Greek words used for **anger**. *Thumos* is the kind of *anger that quickly explodes and then subsides* while *orgilos* is the kind of

anger that a person harbors in his heart. How do you handle your *anger?* Do you blow up (express it in outbursts of rage) or clam up (hold it all in and cry it out later)? _____

_____

Explain what the following verses teach about improper handling of **anger**.

James 1:19-20 _____

_____

Proverbs 14:17, 29 _____

_____

Ecclesiastes 7:9 _____

_____

6. **Not given to wine**: The true leader must not have the character of an uncontrolled, outrageous drunk. One Bible scholar said that the *wine* most commonly drunk in Paul's day was either nonalcoholic or had very low alcohol content. Fermented juice was mixed with water (8 or 10 parts water to 1 part wine) to lessen its power to intoxicate. Because water was frequently contaminated, as it is in many third world countries today, the slight alcohol content acted as a disinfectant to the water. Why would you (or would you not) drink a couple beers with your friends?_____

_____

Drinking leads to wrong friends, dangerous parties, and ruined testimonies. What are some of the results of drinking taught in passages like Isaiah 28:7-8 and Proverbs 23:29-35? _____

_____

7. **No striker**: Leaders are not belligerent, argumentative, violent men who go around looking for a fight. Who do you know that is constantly on the edge of a verbal or physical fight? _____

_____

Would anyone go to that kind of person for spiritual help? _____

In contrast to a **striker**, how does 2 Timothy 2:24-25 describe the traits of a true leader?

_____

8. **Not given to filthy lucre**: Godly leaders are not greedy! I heard of a dad who answered his college son's request for money, "I am enclosing the $10 you requested in your letter. Incidentally, $10 is spelled with one zero, not two!" A love for money reveals a discontented heart. What warning did Paul give in 1 Timothy 6:5-12 about riches? _____

_____

> According to Titus 1:7, how can we learn to be blameless
> and not self-centered in our personal life?

13

Thursday

LEADERS NEED TO BE BLAMELESS (NOT SELF-CENTERED) IN THEIR PUBLIC LIFE
Titus 1:8

But a lover of hospitality, a lover of good men, sober, just, holy, temperate.

Titus 1:7 dealt with the negatives of a leader's character; verse 8 lists six positive character traits. Whether or not you will ever be in full-time Christian work, you really should strive to have these characteristics in your life. To win your unsaved community to Christ, you must have a public testimony that is blameless and above reproach.

1. **Lover of hospitality**: You can tell what a person is like on the inside by what he loves and hates on the outside. The phrase **lover of hospitality** does not mean that you love to visit hospitals. It describes *a friendly, hospitable lover of strangers.* We all are comfortable around our circle of friends and are often hesitant to reach out of that comfort zone to other people, especially people we don't know. Who in your youth group or church reaches out to visitors? _____

When you show **love** to a stranger, you are giving to someone you may never see again, which means you are giving without expecting anything in return. That's true biblical **love**. What does Matthew 25:34-40 say about **loving** strangers? _____

_____

2. **Lover of good (men)**: This phrase could mean either **good men** or simply **good**. We live in a world where people seem to **love** what is bad and hate what is **good**! Below are verses that deal with **good** and bad. After each reference, write the verbs that deal with the **good**, then the verbs that deal with the "bad."

Amos 5:15a _____

Romans 12:9_____

1 Thessalonians 5:15 _____

1 Thessalonians 5:21-22 _____

3. **Sober**: In Titus 2:2 *sober* is translated *temperate* and in Titus 2:5 it is translated *discreet.* The Greek word *sophron* has the idea of *being safe and sound in mind or self-controlled in thinking.* It is a picture of the sensible guy who is balanced and avoids extravagance or overindulgence. We are generally known and remembered for our extremes. If we are not careful, extremes can draw the attention to ourselves and away from our Lord. If we are known for any extreme, it should be an extreme love for God and an extreme hatred for sin. What extremes are you known for?_____

_____

If there is an imbalance in any area of your life, where would it be? _____

_____

What can you do to have the testimony of being *sober*? _____

_____

4. **Just**: From the word **just** we get words like justice and justifiable, but in the Bible it is most often translated *righteous.* If a person is known for being **just** or *righteous*, most would assume he would "do right" no matter what! We can learn much from this word.

Match the reference with the truth below.

Matthew 23:28	There is a difference between the just and the wicked.
Matthew 27:19	Some pretend to be just and righteous.
Mark 6:20	Jesus was known to be a just man.
Ephesians 6:1	John the Baptist was a just man.
James 5:16	Just men know how to pray.
1 John 3:12	Even kids can be just and righteous.

5. **Holy**: A true, spiritual leader must not be outwardly religious only, but *inwardly right in his relationship with God.* We can all fake it at times. Our reputation is what people think we are; our character is what God knows us to be. What is necessary to keep a right relationship with God? _____

_____

_____

What two things does James encourage us to do in James 4:8 that help us stay close to our Lord?

_____

6. **Temperate**: This word comes from a root word meaning *strong or mighty.* A leader who is **temperate** is *strong in his self-control or self-discipline.* A leader who does not keep an eye on his secret life or does not keep a clear conscience by constantly seeking forgiveness and grace, is not self-controlled. Our strength to say "no" to sin and "yes" to God is really not in ourselves, but in the power God offers to us. The root word for **temperate** is found in the following three verses. Fill in the remainder of these verses.

Ephesians 1:19 _____

_____ His mighty power.

Ephesians 6:10 _____

_____ power of His might.

Colossians 1:11 _____

_____His glorious power,

_____

7. We have studied six characteristics of a godly leader: **lover of hospitality**, **lover of good**, **sober-minded**, **just**, **holy**, and self-controlled. As you examine your own heart, which of these traits are you the strongest in?

_____

Which are you the weakest in? _____

_____

According to Titus 1:8, how can we learn to be blameless
and not self-centered in our public life?

Friday
LEADERS NEED TO BE BLAMELESS (NOT SELF-CENTERED) IN THEIR PREACHING.
Titus 1:9

....

Holding fast the faithful Word as he hath been taught, that he may be able by sound doctrine both to exhort and to convince the gainsayers.

....

Godly leadership is based on a commitment to the **Word of God**. A true leader must never fall into the trap of trusting in his gifts or personality but must fully trust **God's Word** to change lives. Titus 1:9 emphasizes the fact that the Bible has the answers to all the problems we will face in life.

1. Have you ever watched a small child hold onto a toy and not let go even though another child is trying to take it away? This is something like what the term **holding fast** means. This phrase means *to strongly cling or adhere to or to be super-glued to*. An individual "super-glued" to God's Word is one who is unquestionably loyal and committed to the Bible. Rating yourself from 1 to 10, how committed are you to the **Word of God**?_____

What word is repeated four times in Colossians 4:16?_____

Rate yourself on how committed are you to reading **God's Word**. _____

Write out Psalm 119:11. _____

_____

Again rate yourself on how committed you are to memorizing the Bible. _____

According to Joshua 1:8, how often should we meditate on the **Word of God**? _____

How would you rate your commitment to meditating on Scripture? _____

Read Deuteronomy 11:26-28. Who did God promise to bless?_____

Who did God promise to curse? _____

Rate yourself on your commitment to obeying the **Word of God**._____

Holding fast God's faithful Word means you have a super-glued commitment to reading, memorizing, meditating on, and obeying **God's Word**.

2. Paul mentioned that this **faithful Word** had been taught. List four individuals who have impacted your life through their teaching or preaching of **God's Word**. _____

_____

Have you ever considered surrendering your life to teach or preach the **Word of God**? _____

If you have or are praying about it, which type of ministry (pastor, missionary, evangelist, teacher, youth pastor, or writer) would you prefer and why? _____

_____

3. Paul reminded Titus that it was **sound doctrine** that enabled him to minister to the young Christians in Crete. According to one Bible commentator, the idea of teaching **doctrine** that is **sound** simply refers *to doctrine that is healthy and wholesome, directed at protecting and preserving life*. The word **sound** is used as an adjective five times in the epistle of Titus. Fill in the blanks below.

Titus 1:9 sound _____ Titus 1:13 sound _____ Titus 2:1 sound_____

Titus 2:2 sound _____ Titus 2:8 sound _____

4. Anytime you hear of a preacher or minister attacking the purity of the Gospel by adding to God's simple plan of salvation or taking away from it, you avoid them and warn others about them. Do you know anyone who teaches that a person needs to be baptized in order to be saved? _____

How does that teaching violate Ephesians 2:8-9? _____

Have you ever heard someone preach that repentance is not necessary for salvation? _____

How does that disagree with Luke 13:3, Acts 3:19, Romans 2:4, and 2 Corinthians 7:9-10? _____

_____

5. A pastor, or any Christian, who loves **the faithful Word** respects it, believes it, studies it, preaches it, and lives it. Do your beliefs affect your decisions in life? _____

How well do you practice what you preach? _____

Can you think of two areas that you really need to change? _____

_____

6. Pastors are often compared with shepherds. One commentator said that "a pastor needs two voices: one for gathering sheep and the other for driving away wolves and thieves." What do you think the word **exhort** means?_____

What do you think **convince** means? _____

Exhort has the idea of *comfort or encouragement* where **convince** has the thought of *convicting, rebuking, or telling of a fault*. Circle the references below that encourage us to **exhort** others and underline the ones that teach us to confront.

Ephesians 5:11   1 Timothy 5:20   Hebrews 3:13   2 Corinthians 1:4

Romans 12:1   James 2:9   Revelation 3:19

7. **Gainsayers** are *those who oppose, contradict, or want to argue with the truth*. It literally means "to talk back." Do you know anyone that just loves to argue? _____

By the way, teens who "talk back" to their parents are a type of **gainsayers**. That displeases God! In order to win over a **gainsayer**, you need to have a good grasp on the application of God's Word. Do you know the Bible well enough to refute someone who wants to argue about movies, television, or rock music?

_____

How can a consistent Scripture memory plan help you prepare for this? _____

I have put together a booklet called *Five Smooth Stones Scripture Memory Plan* that could be a great help in this area. You can contact THE WILDS to get information how to get it. Daily memorize the Bible and you will be prepared to help those arguing **gainsayers** you face.

> According to Titus 1:9, how can we learn to be blameless
> and not self-centered in sharing God's Word with others?

17

SATURDAY REVIEW
Titus 1:1-6

According to Titus 1:1-4, how did Paul personally attack SELF-CENTEREDNESS?

According to Titus 1:5-6, how can leaders be blameless and not SELF-CENTERED in their family life?

SUNDAY REVIEW

Titus 1:7-9

According to Titus 1:7, how can we learn to be blameless and not SELF-CENTERED in our personal life?

According to Titus 1:8, how can we learn to be blameless and not SELF-CENTERED in our public life?

According to Titus 1:9, how can we learn to be blameless and not SELF-CENTERED in sharing God's Word with others?

Monday
SHUTTING THE MOUTHS OF REBELLIOUS TEACHERS
Titus 1:10-11

For there are many unruly and vain talkers and deceivers, specially they of the circumcision: Whose mouths must be stopped, who subvert whole houses, teaching things which they ought not, for filthy lucre's sake.

Unlike the faithful leaders in the first part of this chapter, Titus 1:10-11 deals with the character, motives, and behavior of rebellious, false teachers. Much of what Titus faced on Crete we have to face today. Let's see how Paul encouraged Titus to deal with people who reject the Bible, make up their own rules for life, and try to get everyone else to live by their opinions. Paul told Titus that their **mouths must be stopped**! This does not sound like a fun job.

THE IDENTITY OF THE REBELLIOUS TEACHERS

1. What word in Titus 1:10 gives an idea of how many rebellious **deceivers** Titus had to contend with?

_____

In your experience, which is more popular: being worldly or being godly? _____

If we choose to follow the crowd, would we be following the majority or the minority? _____

What do the following verses say about mixing in or standing alone?

Exodus 23:2 _____

_____

Joshua 24:15 _____

_____

1 Samuel 15:24 _____

_____

Proverbs 1:10-11, 15_____

_____

2. The word **unruly** is probably the best word to describe these *deceivers*. It has the meaning of *total rebellion, a refusal to obey any and all authority, a refusal to submit to any law or leader.* Those who are **unruly** *refuse to be disciplined by themselves or others.*

Can you think of anyone you know personally who would be considered **unruly**? _____

Would your parents or any of your authorities consider you **unruly**? _____

Being **unruly** is about as proud and self-centered as anyone can get. What does God have to say about proud, selfish individuals in James 4:6 and 1 Peter 5:5?_____

_____

3. **Vain talkers** are *empty individuals who have nothing of value to say.* It is not that they do not talk, but what they say is worthless. What does James 1:26 say about those who cannot control what they say?

4. **Deceivers** *emotionally attack people's minds in hopes of turning them away from the truth. They reject God's requirements on their lives and think they can believe and live as they wish.* Have any of your friends ever tried to deceive or trick you into believing that sin is OK and won't hurt anyone? _____ Be not deceived!

THE INFLUENCE OF THE REBELLIOUS TEACHERS

5. **Who subvert whole houses**: This phrase tells us why Paul put such an emphasis on shutting the mouths of the rebellious teachers. The word **subvert** means *to overturn or overthrow.* These guys encouraged entire families to believe a lie! Why? For money or whatever they could get out of the situation. What religions or denominations have you seen or heard about that spend more time begging for money than serving God's people? _____

Those who constantly ask for money often stretch or twist Scripture. They give false promises like, "God will give you five times what you gave Him." Now God might, but He does not say that in His Word.

6. **Teaching things which they ought not**: There is much preached in the name of God that **ought not** be preached or taught. What does 1 Timothy 5:13 call those who **speak things which they ought not**? ___

_____

Below are listed five **ought nots**. Think of three more that you could add to the list and write them in the space provided.

We **ought not** preach or teach any Gospel that says you must earn or work your way to God.

We **ought not** preach or teach a "1-2-3 repeat after me, if you haven't done it do it," non-repentive, easy-believism type of salvation.

We **ought not** preach or teach our preferences as convictions.

We **ought not** preach or teach about a God we've tried to bring down to our level by throwing a pair of Levis on Him rather than preaching about a holy, powerful, sin hating God.

We **ought not** preach or teach anything that is divisive or separates God-loving, God-fearing believers.

_____

_____

_____

7. **For filthy lucre's sake**: **Filthy lucre** is referring *to money or wealth gained in a shameful or dishonest way.* What does 1 Timothy 6:9 say will happen to those who will or desire to be rich? _____

_____

What does 1 Timothy 6:10 say is the root of all evil? _____

_____

From the same verse, what happens to those individuals who greedily lust or covet after money?

_____

Do you struggle with wanting more and more things? _____

Extreme self-centeredness is seen in people who, like the false teachers, will do anything for money. May the same never be said of you.

> What did you learn from Titus 1:10-11 that can help you silence false
> teaching that leads to a SELF-CENTERED (not a CHRIST-CENTERED) life?

Tuesday
Dealing with ravenous, selfish, lazy liars
Titus 1:12

....

One of themselves, even a prophet of their own, said, The Cretians are alway liars, evil beasts, slow bellies.

....

The Cretian **prophet** Paul was referring to in Titus 1:12 was a highly respected, sixth-century B.C. poet named Epimenides. Historians say he was considered to be one of the seven great wise men of Greece. His statement about the Cretians may have been made in a general way, but it was obvious that many of them had such a reputation. The late Evangelist Bob Jones Sr. once said, "Your character is what God knows you to be; your reputation is what men think you are." [1]

1. Describe your personal reputation or what most of your friends or family think about you. _____

_____

What areas of character are you strongest in? _____

What areas of character do you struggle with the most? _____

How well does your reputation match your character? _____

Why is it so important that both your public life and your private life should be patterned after our Lord Jesus Christ? _____

2. Whether or not Epimenides was exaggerating or speaking in generalities, his use of the word **alway** was not wise. Obviously, not every man in Crete was this way or Titus would not have been able to ordain any elders or spiritual leaders on that island. All-inclusive words like "always" and "never" should be avoided in conversation, especially in the middle of an argument or disagreement.
Do you catch yourself saying things like, "You NEVER care about anyone but yourself!" or "You ALWAYS interrupt me when I am talking!" _____

Because the "always and never" statements cannot be proven, they only seem to heat up an argument, and they are usually exaggerations, it is not wise to use them.

3. **Who wants to be called a LIAR?** Not me! And probably not you! *Liars* are about as self-centered as you can get. According to Proverbs 26:28, what does a **liar** think of the ones he lies to?_____

_____

What kind of individuals hate lying in Proverbs 13:5? _____

According to Psalm 119:163, what should be our attitudes towards lying? _____

What does Ephesians 4:25 say we should do with lying?_____

According to Proverbs 14:5, who will not lie, and who will lie?_____

What are we commanded not to do in Colossians 3:9? _____

According to Titus 1:2, can God lie? _____

What lie is mentioned in 1 John 1:6?_____

_____

According to John 8:44, who is the father of lies?_____

List four of the individuals listed with the *liars* in Revelation 21:8. _____

_____

4. **Who wants to be called an evil beast?** The Cretians had the reputation of being like vicious, venomous wild **beasts** that lived only to satisfy their own intense appetites. Comparing people with animals is not uncommon even today. Those who struggle with laziness or sloppiness are compared to a lazy pig or a big, fat hog. If a guy or a girl act a little bit spacy, they are considered squirrelly. Some are as strong as an ox, sing like a nightingale, or eat like a bird. If you had to compare yourself with some animal, what would it be and why? _____

_____

The **evil beasts** of Titus 1:12 are describing those *who are totally absorbed with self, wanting only to satisfy their own appetites.* Can you think of three superstars, rock stars, professional athletes, or politicians who are known for their incredible wickedness and appetite for sex, drugs, or alcohol?

_____

_____

5. **Who wants to be called a slow belly?** When Epimenides mentioned the **slow bellies**, he was probably referring to *inactive, lazy, useless men who refused to work or hold down a job.* Basically, he could have called them lazy bums. What does God have to say about laziness in the following verses?

Proverbs 24:30-34 _____

_____

Proverbs 26:13-15 _____

_____

Romans 12:11 _____

_____

Would someone in your family call you lazy? _____

Would you rather be known for being lazy or diligent? _____

What can you do to have the kind of character that results in a diligent reputation? _____

_____

What did you learn about truthfulness, selfishness, and diligence from Titus 1:12 that can help you become more CHRIST-CENTERED and less SELF-CENTERED today?

Wednesday
REBUKING THE EAR-SCRATCHERS
Titus 1:13-14

....

This witness is true. Wherefore rebuke them sharply, that they may be sound in the faith; Not giving heed to Jewish fables, and commandments of men, that turn from the truth.

....

1. Titus 1:13-14 tells us what to do with the selfish, lazy liars we learned about in verse 12. Our ultimate goal is to help them, even if they do not want our help. Verse 13 begins with the phrase, **this witness is true.** Paul did not spend his time spreading vicious rumors that could not be proven. What Epimenides said about the Cretians was true. Before we start repeating gossip or rumors about someone, we had better find out the truth. What do the following verses have to say regarding rumors, gossip, and talebearers?

Proverbs 18:8 _____

_____

Proverbs 11:13 _____

_____

Proverbs 25:9 _____

_____

1 Timothy 5:13 _____

_____

2. Because the testimony of the Cretians was true, Titus was encouraged to **rebuke them sharply.** The word **rebuke** means *to reprove, confront, or tell someone what is wrong in their life.* No one loves being rebuked, but it is actually God's way of keeping us from messing up our lives. When was the last time you were **rebuked** about something in your life? _____

Did you get defensive or try to keep a good attitude and accept the criticism? _____

What do Proverbs 5:12-13 and Proverbs 12:1 say about loving and hating reproof? _____

_____

Some think that anyone who confronts or **rebukes** others is uncaring and mean. How does Revelation 3:19 refute that thought? _____

_____

What is the main reason or purpose for **rebuking** someone according to 1 Timothy 5:20 and Titus 1:13?

_____

_____

3. Titus' goal for the lazy false teachers was *that they may be sound in the faith.* As one commentator says, he was not sent to condemn these men but to correct them with the spirit of patience and gentleness. In a way, they are sick. They teach and live by a weak, unhealthy, and sickly philosophy of life. We are not to attack them but to admonish them. Our goal is not to destroy them but to rescue them from the false teaching. How can this apply to a friend at church or school who is constantly trying to get you involved in some things that you know both your parents and God are against? _____

_____

4. **Not giving heed to Jewish fables, and commandments of men, that turn from the truth**: These *fables* and *commandments* are man-made. Here are two commentators' explanations of what Paul is referring to. For several centuries, Jewish rabbis had been developing many traditional laws, identified here as the **commandments of men**. Those **commandments** probably referred to, and certainly included, legalistic ordinances and standards—most of them doubtless from the Talmud—that added to and often contradicted or nullified Scripture. [2]

The word used here gives the sense of silly **fables**, fictions, or stories that were not founded on fact. The pagan religion abounded with fictions of this kind, and the Jewish teachers were also remarkable for the number of such **fables** which they had introduced into their system. It is probable that the apostle referred here particularly to the **Jewish fables**, and the counsel which he gives is to have nothing to do with them. [3]

5. What does it mean, to **turn from the truth**? Living in the self-centered, postmodern world that we live in automatically puts us face-to-face with relativism. Many believe that if they believe something, it is **truth**! Some think that **truth** is relative to the individual and situation, NOT based on the absolute **truth** of God's Word. They only trust in that which is right in their own eyes.

What absolute **truth** does John 14:6 teach? _____

What absolute **truth** does John 3:16-18 teach? _____

What absolute **truth** does Romans 3:10, 23 teach?_____

What absolute **truth** does Romans 5:18 teach? _____

What absolute **truth** does Acts 3:19 teach? _____

What absolute **truth** does Romans 10:9-10 teach? _____

What absolute **truth** does Romans 10:13 teach?_____

Never allow anyone to **turn you from the truth** of God's Word. Read it, believe it, trust it, and obey it. There is absolute **truth** and it is called the **Bible**.

What did you learn about rebuke and truth from Titus 1:13-14 that can help you be more CHRIST-CENTERED and less SELF-CENTERED today?

Thursday
UNTO THE PURE ALL THINGS ARE PURE.
Titus 1:15

....

Unto the pure all things are pure: but unto them that are defiled and unbelieving is nothing pure; but even their mind and conscience is defiled.

....

For centuries, this verse has been widely used by Christians to defend selfish and sinful behavior. In today's schools, teachers often teach that things are relative. Relativism says that truth is whatever people want it to be. If someone thinks certain behavior is **pure**, then it must be **pure**. If someone thinks certain activities are wicked, then they must be. Many people believe that whatever someone THINKS is actually the truth. To combat this error, Paul is helping Titus deal with the early-church problem of adding rules and regulations to God's Word and legalistically setting standards for the church, especially in regards to dietary laws and regulations. Below is a simple explanation of this verse by a modern-day commentator.

> Dietary laws and asceticism were key doctrines to false teachers, and Paul attacked these people in Titus 1:15. It is unfortunate that Titus 1:15 has been so grossly abused by misinformed Christians. Some Christians use it to support their own sinful practices, saying, "**To the pure, all things are pure**—so what I am doing is not wrong." Paul had nothing of this sort in mind when he dictated these words. He was dealing with the problem of clean and unclean foods, as he had in 1 Timothy 4:2-5. He is teaching that the believer who knows the Word of God receives all foods as clean; the unbeliever (and the false teacher) has a defiled mind and conscience and therefore sees nothing as pure. In fact, instead of the impure foods defiling the heretic, he defiles the food! Moral purity is not a matter of diets; it is a matter of a clean heart and a good conscience. Jesus taught this in Matthew 6:22-23. [4]

1. How would you define legalism?_____

_____

What is the difference between someone who is a legalist and someone who believes in personal holiness and tries to separate from worldly influence and entertainment? _____

_____

Those who base their spirituality and relationship with God on what they do or what they don't do are legalistic in their thinking. They think they can earn favor with God by doing or not doing something. God loved us even when we were unsaved and unforgiven. Can anyone "earn" favor with God?_____

What does Ephesians 2:8-9 teach about how God forgave us and saved us? _____

_____

According to 1 Peter 1:15-16, why are we to live holy lives? _____

_____

Living a holy and separated life does not mean we throw a pair of Levis on Jesus and bring Him down to our level, but we view God as a holy God and we seek to be like Him! Rating yourself from 1 to 10, how holy is your personal life? _____

2. How do we choose between right and wrong without falling into a legalistic mindset? Here is a list of four questions we need to ask when facing any controversial situation. Write out each passage on the following page and explain how each passage supports each question.

Is it BIBLICAL? Does God's Word command it or speak expressly for it?

2 Timothy 3:14-17 _____

_____

_____

James 1:22-25 _____

_____

_____

Is it BAD? Does God's Word forbid it or speak directly against it?

Romans 12:9 _____

_____

_____

James 1:14-16 _____

_____

_____

Is it BINDING? Can you be brought into bondage to it? Can you become so enslaved and addicted that it controls what you do and who you are?

2 Peter 2:19 _____

_____

_____

Romans 6:16 _____

_____

_____

Is it BEST? Some issues are hard to discern. Ask yourself if the activity is the best way to help you serve God, serve others, and stay away from temptation.

1 Corinthians 6:12 _____

_____

_____

1 Corinthians 10:23 _____

_____

_____

What did you learn about legalism and holiness from Titus 1:15 that can help you be more CHRIST-CENTERED and less SELF-CENTERED today?

Friday

SOME ARE PROFESSORS, BUT NOT POSSESSORS.
Titus 1:16

....

They profess that they know God; but in works they deny Him, being abominable, and disobedient, and unto every good work reprobate.

....

1. **They profess that they know God**: What Paul is saying about the rebellious, false teachers in Titus 1:16 could be said of many **professing** believers today—maybe even some of your friends. First of all, just because someone **professes** to know God does not mean that they do. What did the **professing** believers in Matthew 7:22 do to earn God's favor? _____

What did the Lord tell them in Matthew 7:23? _____

What does Matthew 7:21-22 teach about those who **profess** they know God but really do not? _____

_____

What did Isaiah say about professors who were not possessors in Isaiah 29:13-14? _____

_____

2 Timothy 3:5-9 describes these false professors and gives us a warning. How are we to respond to those who *deny* what they say with their lives? _____

_____

According to the references below from the Epistle of 1 John, what will be evident in the lives of those who really know God?

1 John 2:3-4 _____

_____

1 John 3:14-15 _____

_____

1 John 3:19-21 _____

_____

1 John 4:13 _____

_____

Matthew 7:21-27 deals with two types of self-deception. Some "say" but do not "do" (as in verses 21-23) and others "hear" but do not "do" (as in verses 24-27). According to Titus 1:16, how did the false professors **deny God**? _____

_____

Is there anything in your life that would make you or others wonder whether or not you are truly saved?

_____

_____

None of us are perfect, always do right, or live like we wish we could. But God's Holy Spirit will give us the deep-rooted assurance that we are truly forgiven. Only you and God know if you are faking this whole Christian thing and never have been truly saved from your sins. What does 2 Corinthians 13:5 encourage us to do in regards to our relationship with God? _____

2. **In works they deny Him**: What we "do" speaks so loudly others cannot hear what we are "saying!" Someone has said, "Our walk talks and our talk talks, but our walk talks louder than our talk talks!" What do you think about people who say they believe in pleasing God, but live completely for self?

_____

_____

What is your definition of a hypocrite? _____

_____

Not only does a phony, hypocritical life lose all respect, but it also accomplishes absolutely nothing in others' lives. What does the following passage say about such a life?

Matthew 23:27-28 **Woe unto you, scribes and Pharisees, hypocrites! for ye are like unto whited sepulchres, which indeed appear beautiful outward, but are within full of dead men's bones, and of all uncleanness. Even so ye also outwardly appear righteous unto men, but within ye are full of hypocrisy and iniquity.**

_____

_____

3. **Being abominable, and disobedient, and unto every good work reprobate**: God called these sorry leaders detestable, **disobedient**, and worthless. Their entire lives deny that they even **know God**. The word for **abominable** is _closely associated with the word abomination which means to hate-hate-hate_. These false teachers pretended that they believed in God, but they did things that God hated, **disobeying** God's commandments. What do you love that God hates?_____

_____

Is there anything in your life that God loves and you either hate or at least don't enjoy doing? ____

_____

Paul is speaking of unbelievers in Titus 1:16. Assuming that you are truly saved, do you allow the characteristics of these rebels to sneak into your life?_____

4. **Unto every good work reprobate** means they were _unfit or disqualified for any good work!_ One sin, especially the sin of immorality, can disqualify any of us from spiritual leadership in the church. Do you know anyone who was in the ministry and disqualified himself because of sin?_____

How much did it hurt his family or church members?_____

_____

How did it affect those around him?_____

_____

> What have you learned about professing Christ and possessing Christ from Titus 1:16 that can help you become more CHRIST-CENTERED and less SELF-CENTERED today?

SATURDAY REVIEW
Titus 1:10-12

What did you learn from Titus 1:10-11 that can help you silence false teaching that leads to a SELF-CENTERED (not a CHRIST-CENTERED) life?

What did you learn about truthfulness, selfishness, and diligence from Titus 1:12 that can help you become more CHRIST-CENTERED and less SELF-CENTERED today?

SUNDAY REVIEW
Titus 1:13-16

What did you learn about rebuke and truth from Titus 1:13-14 that can help you
be more CHRIST-CENTERED and less SELF-CENTERED today?

What did you learn about legalism and holiness from Titus 1:15 that can help
you be more CHRIST-CENTERED and less SELF-CENTERED today?

What have you learned about professing Christ and
possessing Christ from Titus 1:16 that can help you become
more CHRIST-CENTERED and less SELF-CENTERED today?

Monday
MAKING THE WORD OF GOD ATTRACTIVE
Titus 2:1

But speak thou the things which become sound doctrine.

It is quite interesting to watch teenagers and even college-aged couples interact. Much work is done in front of the bathroom mirror preparing for these face-to-face meetings. Now, no one in their right mind wants to date or marry someone who looks like they ran through the ugly forest and never missed a branch. We do what we can to make ourselves look "attractive." Godly leadership does the same with God's Word. Today we will study the importance of using our lives to make simple Bible teaching look attractive in the eyes of an unsaved world.

1. The first and third words of this verse, **but** and **thou,** actually could be said in this way: *Titus, but as for you...!* After spending seven verses in chapter one (Titus 1:10-16) describing the character of selfish, rebellious teachers, Paul reemphasizes to Titus that he is to be different and to live a life in contrast to those phonies. Titus was called to be a spiritual leader on the island of Crete. What is the name of the town, church, or school where God has called you to lead your friends to a stronger spiritual walk with God?

_____

If you are consistently working through this six-week Bible study, it is obvious that you want to learn what you can to be a leader that makes a difference. The only way to make a difference is by being different.

How is a spiritual leader to be different in his prayer life? _____

_____

How is a spiritual leader to be different in his personal Bible study? _____

_____

How is a spiritual leader to be different in his appearance? _____

_____

How is a spiritual leader to be different in his entertainment choices? _____

_____

How is a spiritual leader to be different in his personal holiness?_____

_____

2. The sixth and seventh words of this verse, **which become**, should have a significant impact on *how we apply Bible doctrine to our everyday lives.* The word *become* is from the Greek word *prepo* which refers *to that which towers up, is conspicuous, or draws attention in an attractive way.* In years past, someone would say, "That outfit is very becoming on you." Today we'd simply say, "Wow, you look good in that!" Our lives are to draw attention to the Gospel of Jesus Christ in such a way that the Gospel is attractive in the eyes of the unsaved. How would a person have to look or act to make the Gospel look cheap, meaningless, or fake? _____

_____

What kind of behavior would give the Gospel a worldly appearance?_____

_____

What word does Titus 2:10 use that helps explain this concept? _____

3. The Greek word for **doctrine** has the idea of *learning, teaching, or instruction.* Bible **doctrine** is not a scary, ultra-academic class that can only be taught in colleges or seminaries. Bible **doctrine** is simply what the Bible teaches! In many **doctrine's** books, huge words are used to describe the various teachings. For instance, the **doctrine** of Eschatology is what the Bible teaches about the end times. The **doctrine** of Soteriology is what the Bible teaches about salvation. Even though we may not be able to pronounce the big words, we can understand what God's Word teaches. What do you believe will happen when the Lord returns in the rapture? _____

_____

What Scripture do you use to support what you believe? _____

What do you believe about salvation? What happens in a person's heart when they get saved? _____

_____

What Scripture do you use to support what you believe? _____

_____

4. **Sound doctrine***:* The word *sound* is from a word that means *healthy or whole.* Healthy Bible teaching produces healthy Christian lives. We live in a time where most people do not want straightforward preaching of absolute truth from the Word of God. What does 2 Timothy 4:3-4 say people want or do not want? _____

_____

According to 1 Timothy 1:10, what kind of lifestyles contradict **sound doctrine**? _____

_____

How was Titus supposed to use **sound doctrine** to deal with the rebellious and unruly false teachers in Titus 1:9? _____

_____

How can **sound doctrine** help you take a stand against peer pressure and the wrong kind of friends?

_____

_____

How can **sound doctrine** help you keep a strong personal relationship with God? _____

_____

What have you learned from Titus 2:1 that can help you make the Gospel look attractive by living a CHRIST-CENTERED (not a SELF-CENTERED) life?

Tuesday
DIGNIFIED, ELDERLY GENTLEMEN
Titus 2:2

That the aged men be sober, grave, temperate, sound in faith, in charity, in patience.

A handsome picture of the Word of God in action is a group picture of elderly men who for years have sought God with their whole hearts. These men in their 60s, 70s, and 80s are sensible gentlemen who are not known for their extremes, but for their balance. They are dignified gentlemen who are worthy of respect because of their obvious discernment and discretion. They are men who are known for their strong self-control and disciplined lives. Although their physical health may be weakening, their faith and trust in God's total control, their apparent love for God and others and their incredible endurance are more healthy than ever.

1. **The aged men**: What is old? _____

Some teens think that anyone over thirty should get free coffee at McDonald's with their senior citizen discount. The word used for **aged** in the ancient Greek often referred *to those in their sixties or above, but was also used for those as young as fifty.* What is old to you? _____

What kind of attitude should you have towards the elderly folks in your church? _____

In what ways can you serve them? _____

_____

Throughout Scripture we see that old age was held in honor and respect. What does Leviticus 19:32 teach about a proper view of the elderly? _____

_____

What do Genesis 15:15, Exodus 20:12, Job 5:26, and Psalm 91:16 teach in common? _____

_____

Write out Job 12:12. _____

_____

List the names of three elderly people you know who personally have had a great impact on your life.

_____

Now, list three life principles you have learned from elderly friends. _____

_____

_____

As we study the characteristics of a godly, elderly man, we need to grow in each of these areas so that when we get old, we can have a testimony that pleases God and is a blessing to others.

2. **Sober**: What is the first thing you think about when you hear the word **sober**? _____

_____

Being **sober** is *not just refusing to get drunk with alcohol, but the word literally describes a sensibly thinking and balanced guy. It is someone who is not extreme.* As mentioned earlier in our study, we are generally known and remembered for our extremes. If we are known for any extremes, it should be an extreme love for God and an extreme hatred for sin. What are you known for? _____

_____

Are you known for any extremes that could hurt your testimony? _____

_____

What do you need to start doing in order to "grow old" and have a godly testimony that is not overshadowed by extremes? _____

_____

3. **Grave**: Obviously the word **grave** here is not referring to the place they will put your coffin someday. How would you define the word **grave**? _____

_____

Think of an older man in your church who is *a well-respected, dignified gentlemen.* That's who you can call **grave**. Because of their years of experience (sometimes the difficult experiences of cancer, divorce, or the death of a loved one), they know what is important and do not get caught up with trivial misunderstandings and worthless selfishness. How does 1 Timothy 3:8 and 11 describe a **grave** individual? _____

_____

4. **Temperate**: Godly men who are **temperate** set *a self-controlled, disciplined example for others to follow.* Do you know anyone who is "out-of-control" in the things they say and do? _____

Self-control is essential when you are tempted to blow up at a friend for something they said. Self-control is essential for a pure thought life. Self-control is essential when you are tempted to waste your money. Think of two people: one who lives totally "out-of-control" and one who lives with self-control. As you examine each of their lives, which one are you personally the most like? _____

Which would you rather be like? _____

_____

5. **Sound in faith, love, and patience**: All of us would love to have healthy, childlike faith that is not plagued with doubt or distrust. Write out Romans 10:17. _____

_____

What book of the Bible would you go to for help with the assurance of your salvation? _____

What chapter in 1 Corinthians teaches us the godly way to love? _____

What book gives the story of a man of *patience*? _____

Sound is the opposite of "sick." Sick **faith** is faith plus works; sick **love** is actually lust; sick **patience** complains and says, "Why me?" In what way could your personal **faith**, **love**, or **patience** be considered "sick" or unhealthy? _____

What did you learn from Titus 2:2 that will help you to someday be a dignified, elderly person striving to live a CHRIST-CENTERED (not a SELF-CENTERED) life?

35

Wednesday
GODLY, ELDERLY LADIES
Titus 2:3

....

The aged women likewise, that they be in behaviour as becometh holiness, not false accusers, not given to much wine, teachers of good things.

....

A beautiful picture of God's Word in action is that of elderly women in the church who are known for their conspicuous holy behavior. These ladies refuse to be known as gossips and have become faithful, dedicated teachers in everyday life situations. Over a cup of tea they encourage a new generation of girls to love their husbands and their children without expecting anything in return. A day shopping the outlet malls becomes a classroom where advanced courses in self-control, purity, kindness, servant-hearted home care, and unpopular submission is taught. These elderly saints love God and His Word so much that they pour their lives into active moms and young brides, encouraging them to live God's way so that no one can call God's truth foolish, outdated, or worthless.

1. **The aged women**: In a world where disrespect for elders is increasing, Paul encourages Titus to teach the elderly women to live **holy** lives. List three elderly women who have had an impact on your life and explain how they influenced you for good. _____

_____

2. **Likewise**: The **likewise** goes back to verse one and the phrase **become sound doctrine**. There is never a time in our Christian experience that we can say we have arrived. Even grandmothers are capable of selfishness and sin. In what areas of life do you think elderly women may struggle to "practice what they preach"? _____

_____

3. The phrase **as becometh holiness** has the idea of *a sacred life that is as conspicuous as a castle tower.* What characteristics have you seen in the elderly women you know that make it evident they have hearts that are **holy** and pure toward God? _____

_____

Which of those characteristics would you like to see increase in your life? _____

_____

4. **Not false accusers**: The Greek word for **false accusers** is *diabolos*. This word is used once in 1 Timothy 3:11 as slanderers, once in 2 Timothy 3:3 as false accusers, and thirty-five times in the New Testament as devil. In context, if there is ever a time women act like the devil, it is when *they start talking too much about other people or accuse them of something they are not sure is true.*

Have you ever been GOSSIPED about? _____

How does it feel when someone says something about you that you know is simply not true? _____

_____

According to Titus 2:7-8, what is the best way to gag a gossip? _____

_____

Write a true-to-life story of how gossip has hurt a friend or a false accusation has destroyed a friendship.

_____

_____

_____

_____

5. **Not given to much wine**: **Not given** comes from the word the Greeks used for bondslave and means _to be enslaved or brought into bondage_. The same phrase is used at the end of 2 Peter 2:19 where it says "of the same is he brought into bondage." How can _wine_ or alcoholic beverages enslave someone? Have you ever been around someone who was drunk? _____

How does a drunk, or someone totally under the control of alcohol, behave around other people?

_____

How does Psalm 107:27 describe a drunken man? _____

_____

What four things can you learn about a drunken person from Proverbs 23:29-35?

_____

_____

Why do you think God is displeased with drunkenness? _____

_____

6. **Teachers of good things**: What you learn throughout life needs to be taught to others. Titus was to encourage the older ladies of the church to teach what they learned about **holy** living to the younger ladies. The phrase translated **teachers of good things** is a combination of two words: **teacher** (instructor or master) and **good** (beautiful or virtuous). Who has been a **teacher of good things** to you? _____

_____

What are some of the virtuous, beautiful **good things** that you have learned? _____

_____

List three names of friends that you could _teach the_ **good things** you have been taught by others.

_____

_____

What did you learn from Titus 2:3 that will help you to someday grow old
gracefully and live a CHRIST-CENTERED (not a SELF-CENTERED) life?

Thursday
SPIRITUAL YOUNG WOMEN
Titus 2:4-5

....

That they may teach the young women to be sober, to love their husbands, to love their children, To be discreet, chaste, keepers at home, good, obedient to their own husbands, that the Word of God be not blasphemed.

....

The Christian life is one huge classroom where you never quit learning. Titus 2:4-5 could actually be seen as a list of college-level classes God wants young women to take: Soberness 101, Husband Loving 202, Children Loving 203, Discretion 303, Being Chaste 400, Keepers at Home 500, Being Good 402, Submissive Obedience 600, and Protecting God's Word from Dishonor 703.

1. **Soberness 101:** This class concentrates on learning how to keep your thoughts and mind disciplined and healthy. Explain why misunderstandings, comparisons, jealousies, and discontented spirits could be unhealthy to a disciplined mind. _____

_____

What kind of thoughts does Philippians 4:8 say a disciplined mind should think? _____

_____

_____

2. **Husband Loving 202:** The Greeks combined two words, *philos* and *aner*, to form the phrase **love their husbands**. Together, these two words encourage **young wives** to make **their husbands** their dearest and best friends. What is one way for a wife to show **her husband** that she **loves** him? _____

What usually happens when a wife quits **loving her husband**? _____

List four characteristics of **love** from the list in 1 Corinthians 13:4-7. _____

_____

3. **Children Loving 203:** In much the same way **young wives love their husbands**, they must learn **to love their children**. When Titus taught the elderly ladies to teach the young ladies to p*hiloteknos* **their children**, he was encouraging them *to build fond, loving and encouraging friendships with their own children*. A parent's friendship is the greatest weapon against the peer pressure teens face on a daily basis. According to Proverbs 4:3, how did Solomon feel his mother felt about him? _____

_____

4. **Discretion 303:** Moms and wives need **discretion** *to make the daily "quick decisions"* they face. Proverbs 11:22 gives a strange word picture of moms and **discretion**. Explain what it means.

_____

_____

5. **Being Chaste 400:** When Paul spoke of *hagnos*, the Greek word for **chaste**, he was talking of a girl who was *clean* and *pure* and *innocent*. This purity which is inwardly known by you (and outwardly known by others) should not be confused by your dressing in a way, walking in a way, or talking in a way that would lead someone to question your inward purity. Make sure what others see is what you really are. Don't make them wonder or guess. According to 1 Peter 3:1-2, how can others be affected by your **chaste**, pure, and innocent lifestyle? _____

_____

6. **Keepers at Home 500:** The title to the popular women's magazine seeks to capture the essence of this role: *Good Housekeeping.* A housekeeper is not just a maid who protects her **home** from being overrun by disease, dust, and dirt, but a trained warrior in "keeping" any and all enemies away from her husband and children. The word **keep** in Proverbs 4:23 actually means *to guard.* How can a mom or wife **keep** or *guard* her husband and kids from a wicked world? _____

_____

_____

7. **Being Good 402:** The word used for **being good** means more than just "looking" good, but actually refers *to someone who has a good heart or is good all the way through.* Most of us know the difference between a "good girl" and a "bad girl," and moms are to be known for their **goodness**. Read 1 Peter 3:10-16. How many different ways is the word **good** used in 1 Peter 3:10-16? Explain briefly Peter's idea of **being good**?

_____

8. **Submissive Obedience 600:** Submission is not popular today, for anyone! A godly wife is simply *to accept her God-given role and willingly put herself under the authority of her own husband.* It actually is God's place of protection, not a prison. What do 1 Peter 3:1 and 5 and Ephesians 5:21-22 say about submission? _____

_____

_____

9. **Protecting God's Word from Dishonor 703:** Unbelievers judge the Truth of the Gospel more by what they see us do than what they hear us say. Our lives should make the Gospel message look attractive to others. Does yours? _____

_____

What did you learn from Titus 2:4-5 about how God expects young women to be spiritual and to live a CHRIST-CENTERED (not a SELF-CENTERED) life?

Friday
SELF-CONTROLLED YOUNG MEN
Titus 2:6-8

....

Young men likewise exhort to be sober minded. In all things shewing thyself a pattern of good works: in doctrine shewing uncorruptness, gravity, sincerity, Sound speech, that cannot be condemned; that he that is of the contrary part may be ashamed, having no evil thing to say of you.

....

Every church needs self-controlled **young men**. **Young men**, instead of being impulsive, passionate, ambitious, volatile, and sometimes arrogant, should exercise self-control and show good sense and judgment in all things. Let your life back up what you believe. Be careful what you say so no one can accuse you of attacking others with your words. Be a dignified gentleman with integrity and **sincerity**. Be an example for others to follow, and as an example, lead them directly to Christ.

1. The one major characteristic that seems to overshadow all others in dealing with the **young men** is **sober mindedness**. This is actually a different Greek word than the one used in verse two which meant sensible or discreet. This word has the idea of *healthy, controlled thinking or, in other words, self-control.*

In Mark 5:15, describe the change that took place in the man who was "in his right mind."

_____

_____

From Romans 12:3, what selfish attitude does **sober** thinking attack? _____

2. We live in a world where it is so easy to let your thinking go haywire and completely out-of-control. For just a few more cents you can supersize your fries and drink in most fast-food restaurants. Supersizing a Happy Meal is not really dangerous except for your waistline. On the other hand, supersizing normal desires can literally destroy your life. From 1 John 2:15-17, what three worldly desires does John list?

_____

_____

There are legitimate needs for money, food, sleep, sex (in marriage), and acceptance. But if we let any of these areas totally control our thinking, we are tiptoeing with disaster. Comment on the following three statements below.

• Supersizing your thought-induced desire for money (lust of the eyes) will lead to poor decisions that will eventually tie you down to the world and hinder you from a life of service to God. _____

_____

• Supersizing your thought-induced desire for food, sleep, or sex (lust of the flesh) will lead to slavery to your ever-demanding flesh and cause you to lose focus on others and God. _____

_____

• Supersizing your thought-induced desire for position or popularity (pride of life) will cause you to be a man-pleaser who forgets what it means to be a God-pleaser. _____

3. **In all things showing thyself a pattern**: Little kids love to imitate others. It is a natural thing. We look for models or examples to **pattern** our lives after. Paul encouraged Titus to be that **pattern** for others to follow. If a younger person followed your example, how strong of a testimony would they have?

_____

_____

When Paul said, **in all things**, he was emphasizing the fact that *we cannot pick and choose what we want to be an example in.* List five areas in which you should set a godly example for those younger than you to follow._____

_____

_____

4. The **good works** combined with the **doctrine** form a powerful witness. The combination of the walk and the talk, the visual and the verbal, together make it clear what God says and expects from our lives. Paul gave Titus a list of four godly characteristics that if seen in his life would actually silence his critics. List the four qualities from verses 7-8 in the spaces next to their descriptions.

• _____ Integrity! Something that does not rot, corrupt, or decay. Unlike a delicious-looking shiny, red apple that is rotten on the inside, it is whole and without rot all the way through. A life without rotten spots.

• _____ Sincerity! Genuineness! Real! Authentic! Never false, fake, or pretending. Honest and truthful. Sincere all the way through.

• _____ Dignity! A seriousness or gravity that does not do away with a sense of humor, joy, or laughing. It is knowing when to be serious and when it's OK to be silly. It is knowing what is important and what is not.

• _____ Unblamable speech! Communication that is not filled with lies, hypocrisy, gossip, half-truths, cut-downs, or anger. Those who keep their tongues in control cannot be condemned or falsely accused.

5. Titus 2:8 ends with the phrase, **that he that is of the contrary part may be ashamed, having no evil thing to say of you.** Godly, self-controlled young men are to have a testimony that is unaccusable, unimpeachable, unblamable. How do 1 Peter 2:15 and 3:16 explain this Bible principle? _____

_____

_____

What did you learn from Titus 2:6-8 about how God expects young men to be
self-controlled and to live a CHRIST-CENTERED (not a SELF-CENTERED) life?

SATURDAY REVIEW
Titus 2:1-2

What have you learned from Titus 2:1 that can help you make the Gospel look attractive by living a CHRIST-CENTERED (not a SELF-CENTERED) life?

What did you learn from Titus 2:2 that will help you someday to be a dignified, elderly person striving to live a CHRIST-CENTERED (not a SELF-CENTERED) life?

Sunday Review

Titus 2:3-8

What did you learn from Titus 2:3 that will help you someday to grow old gracefully and to live a CHRIST-CENTERED (not a SELF-CENTERED) life?

What did you learn from Titus 2:4-5 about how God expects young women to be spiritual and to live a CHRIST-CENTERED (not a SELF-CENTERED) life?

What did you learn from Titus 2:6-8 about how God expects young men to be self-controlled and to live a CHRIST-CENTERED (not a SELF-CENTERED) life?

EMPLOYEES THAT BUSINESSES WANT TO HIRE
Titus 2:9-10

....

Exhort servants to be obedient unto their own masters, and to please them well in all things; not answering again; Not purloining, but shewing all good fidelity; that they may adorn the doctrine of God our Saviour in all things.

....

Do we still have *servants* and slaves today? _____

What do you think was the difference between **servants** during Bible times and employees today?

_____

When Paul wrote to Titus, bond-servants were a major part of the workforce and economy. Some were forced into slavery and others chose to serve their masters for a lifetime. Some were abused and mistreated while others were treated as family. Actually, Paul did not give one set of rules for servants with good **masters** and another set of rules for servants with evil **masters**. Paul listed five ways a **servant** could **adorn the doctrine of God**. When you **adorn** yourself (get dressed), do you like to wear clothes that are way too big or way too small? _____

Would you be embarrassed to wear something that has been out-of-date since your parents were teens?

_____

Would you wear stripes with plaids?_____

Would you rather shop at Goodwill or Old Navy®? _____

Would you rather your friends think you "look good" or laugh at you? _____

Although these answers are quite obvious, they do emphasize the principle of **adorning the doctrine of God**. The word **adorn** comes from the Greek word *kosmos* where we get our word cosmetics. Most girls (and some guys) go to their toolboxes (make-up kits) to make themselves look attractive. Our lives, either as slaves, employees, students, or church members, are to dress up the **doctrine of God's Word** or, in other words, make the Bible look good! Here are five ways to truly "look good."

1. **Be obedient unto their own own masters**: Simple **obedience** to authority is a great way to show that you are a Christian. The concept of **obedience** has *the idea of submission or putting yourself under someone else's authority.* Do you like to be told what to do? _____

In a job situation, do you do what you are told? _____

Circle the words in the following verses that could also be translated **obedience**.

- **Submitting yourselves one to another in the fear of God.**
  Ephesians 5:21
- **Wives, submit yourselves unto your own husbands, as unto the Lord.**
  Ephesians 5:22
- **To be discreet, chaste, keepers at home, good, obedient to their own husbands, that the word of God be not blasphemed.**
  Titus 2:5
- **Submit yourselves therefore to God. Resist the devil, and he will flee from you.**
  James 4:7

2. **Please them well in all things**: The phrase **in all things** teaches us that *we cannot pick and choose the ways we want to please those in authority over us.*

Have you ever had a job you really did not like? _____

Have you ever been asked to do things that you felt were beneath you? _____

No matter the request (unless, of course, it is sin) we are to submit to our employers. We are to work in such a way that our employers are *totally satisfied* or **pleased** with our work. Actually, we are to **please** our bosses the same way we seek to *please* God! What does Colossians 3:20 teach is well **pleasing** to God? _____

What does Philippians 4:18 say is well **pleasing** to God? _____

Working hard, with a great attitude, is the best way to **please** both your employer and your Lord. Do you?_____

3. **Not answering again**: Today we would say, *not talking back, not mouthing off, or not sassing*. If we are to give the right picture of a Christian where we work, we had better not have a disrespectful attitude. Have you ever talked back to a boss or a manager? _____

_____

How do the following verses deal with the problem of disrespectfully talking back to those in authority?

Proverbs 30:11_____

Malachi 1:6_____

Ephesians 6:5-7 _____

4. **Not purloining**: **Purloin** sounds more like a type of steak than a type of sin. It is not a word we use today, but it simply means *to steal*. Write out Exodus 20:15. _____

_____

There are many different ways to steal. A student steals by cheating. A thief steals by taking what is not his. An employee steals time by coming to work late, taking too long of a break, or wasting time on the Internet. Have you ever stolen anything? _____

Have you made it right with those you stole from?

_____

What does Ephesians 4:28 say a "former" thief should do? _____

_____

5. **Shewing all good fidelity**: The word **fidelity** is translated *faith* over 225 times in the New Testament. Showing *good faith* expresses *true loyalty*. Loyal employees are the kind of workers that businesses want to hire. Are you a LOYAL worker?_____

_____

What have you learned from Titus 2:9-10 that helps you to be a hard-working, loyal employee who is known for living a CHRIST-CENTERED (not a SELF-CENTERED) life?

Tuesday
Sᴀʟᴠᴀᴛɪᴏɴ ꜰᴏʀ ᴀʟʟ!
Titus 2:11

For the grace of God that bringeth salvation hath appeared to all men.

What a great verse. Talk about hope! This one verse teaches that God gives a universal opportunity for **salvation**. By the way, this is not because we earn it or deserve it, but simply because God wants to give it. Let's take a look at this simple verse and the three incredible truths God wants us to clearly understand.

Fᴏʀ ᴛʜᴇ ɢʀᴀᴄᴇ ᴏꜰ Gᴏᴅ...

Try to define or explain **grace**._____

_____

From the many well-known songs and hymns about **grace**, list the titles of three that you know most of the words to. (If no one is in the room with you, sing one of them!) The **grace of God** mentioned here actually refers *to the very person of Jesus Christ.* Christ is God's gift of *grace.* What phrase from John 3:16 describes this **grace** gift from God? _____

_____

Why was it necessary for Christ to be born sinless and live a sinless life? _____

_____

Did He deserve to die? _____

Did Christ have any sins in His own life to pay for? _____

Why is Christ's death, burial, and resurrection essential for **salvation**? _____

_____

If Christ did not rise from the grave, would Christianity be any different from any other religion in the world? _____

Our eternal destiny rests on this truth: Jesus Christ defeated death. If He had not risen from the dead, we could never be saved from the penalty of our sins. According to Romans 6:23, what is the penalty for sin? _____

Death actually means separation. Eternal death is eternal separation from whom?_____

Hell is the horrible home of no hope. Hell is that place where those who have rejected Jesus Christ's offer of forgiveness will spend eternity separated from God. Who do you personally know that will spend eternity separated from God? _____

What can you do for that individual that might make a difference in his or her eternity? _____

_____

The world, with all its many religions, teaches that we must do something to earn favor with God. **God's grace**, on the other hand, *teaches that we can do nothing to earn God's favor;* He freely gives it to all who trust Him. Write a brief testimony that you would share with one of your unbelieving friends about how God brought you to Himself and **saved** you._____

_____

_____

_____

...THAT BRINGETH SALVATION...

What is **salvation**? _____

_____

Since we all need **salvation**, what is it that we are to be **"saved"** from? _____

Titus 2:11-13 actually shows all three ways we are or will be **saved** from sin. When Paul mentioned *the* **grace of God that bringeth salvation hath appeared to all men** in verse 11, he was talking about our *salvation* from the *Penalty of Sin.* Paul spoke of *salvation* from the *Power of Sin* in verse 12 when he explained that **God's grace** teaches us *that denying ungodliness and worldly lusts, we should live soberly, righteously, and godly, in this present world.* Someday soon we hope to see Jesus Christ return to earth to rapture His church (capture His bride) and **save** us from the *Presence of Sin* as we see in verse 13, **Looking for that blessed hope, and the glorious appearing of the great God and our Saviour Jesus Christ.** Take a minute and thank God for His free gift of **salvation**.

...HATH APPEARED TO ALL MEN.

Jesus has **appeared** and will **appear**. He **appeared** once in His **grace** as a baby in Bethlehem and will **appear** again in His glory as the King of kings and the Lord of lords (1 Timothy 6:15). Just as sure as Jesus Christ **appeared** the first time, He will *appear* again. Just as the Old Testament prophets prophesied that He would be born of a virgin in the city of Bethlehem, so the New Testament prophesies that He will come in His power and glory to rescue His bride from this wicked world. Titus 2:11 is speaking of His first **appearing**. Jesus came to die for all men. What did Paul say in 1 Timothy 2:4? _____

_____

_____

Who is the Gospel available to according to Romans 10:9-13? _____

List two phrases from those verses that teach that **salvation** is available **to all men**. _____

_____

Have you been saved from your sins? _____

Salvation is a free gift from God. Knowing this, we can never be self-centered or proud about our **salvation**. Being Christ-centered is realizing that God did this for us. Thank you, Lord!

> What did you learn from Titus 2:11 about our wonderful gift of salvation that keeps your focus on living a CHRIST-CENTERED (not a SELF-CENTERED) life?

Wednesday
LEARNING FROM THE SCHOOL OF GRACE
Titus 2:12

....

Teaching us that, denying ungodliness and worldly lusts, we should live soberly, righteously, and godly, in this present world.

....

In today's study, we will examine Titus 2:12 to see what can be learned from this "School of Grace." Get your thinking caps on because class is about ready to begin. You are the student and Professor Grace is the teacher.

1. **Teaching us**: The teacher for this course is found in verse 11, **For the grace of God that bringeth salvation hath appeared to all men.** If you remember, this **grace** actually refers *to the very person of Jesus Christ.* Just as our Lord was called Master, or Teacher, by His disciples, we can sit in His classroom and learn just as Peter, Andrew, James, and John learned by sitting at His feet. We have the written Word of God and the living example of the Son of God. Both His life and His Word are the curriculum from which we will learn. Since the Bible is our textbook, how often do you study for life's pop quizzes and tests? Write out 2 Timothy 2:15. _____

_____

_____

When do you have your personal devotions?_____

Where do you have your time with the Lord? _____

What is your set plan as you spend time with God each day? _____

2. **In this present world**: We are to live **sober, righteous, and godly lives in this age** (or **world**) God has placed us in. Some think it would be easier to live in the *Little House on the Prairie* days where all we'd have to deal with would be Nellie's attitude. But God has put us in this technological age with the World Wide Web spun around us. This high-tech age has its share of temptations, but it also offers high-tech opportunities. How can you use a computer to aid in your personal Bible study and research? _____

_____

How can you use high-tech communication to witness to unbelievers? _____

_____

In what way can the Internet be used to encourage missionaries or missionary kids who live outside our own country? _____

How does Romans 12:1-2 encourage us to deal with the **present world** or age we live in? _____

_____

3. In our Titus 2:12 classroom, what two things are we taught to deny? _____

_____

What three ways are we taught to live? _____

_____

4. **Denying ungodliness**: We must learn to say "no" and not "yes" to selfish, **ungodly** thinking. We must also learn to say "no" to wicked, irreverent, **ungodly** people. Do you have any friends or acquaintances that try to pressure you into sin? _____

Is there anyone at your school or work who lives a very wicked life and loves to see others get involved with his or her sin?_____

In Romans 1:18, what is God's anger revealed against? _____

How many times is the word ungodly used in Jude 15? _____

We do not have to fear God's judgment if we refuse to live **ungodly** lives.

5. **Denying worldly lusts**: **Worldly desires** are *sins that we want to commit even if we never have.* **Lust** is *simply an intense passion or desire, often for something God never intended us to have.* How does 2 Timothy 2:22 describe these **lusts**? _____

_____

What does 1 Peter 2:11 say about them? _____

How are they described in 1 Timothy 6:9?_____

According to Galatians 5:16, how can we say "no" to these fleshly **lusts**? _____

_____

6. **Living soberly**: We are to live with a mind under control and a thought life that pleases God. This is not always easy, but it is possible as we discipline ourselves to "put in" God's Word and "put out" selfish and sensual thinking. What type of thinking does Paul deal with in Romans 12:3 where he also uses the phrase **think soberly**? _____

_____

Along with vigilance, what does Peter say is necessary to be on constant guard against the devil?

_____

This is not the first time Paul mentions the word sober to Titus. What other verses have we already studied that use this word? (Hint: It is used once in chapter one and three times in chapter two.) _____

_____

7. **Living righteously**: The word **righteous** in this verse refers *to someone who is honest, just and fair.* They are not crooked or one-sided. You can always trust them. God is a **righteous** judge. Who do you know that is just and fair?_____

Would your friends say you were **righteous**? _____

8. **Living godly**: **Godliness** is not simply doing godly things; it is *a mindset and a way of life.* **Godliness** is actually CHRIST-CENTEREDness! A **godly** life is *devoted to God and dependent on God.* It is the opposite of self-centeredness, which is a life totally wrapped up with self. If you were to rate yourself on a scale where one is self-centered and ten is CHRIST-CENTERED, how would you score?_____

Are you pleased with that rating? _____ Is God pleased? _____

> How has Titus 2:12 impacted your life and helped you to say "no" to sin and "yes"
> to God as you seek to live a CHRIST-CENTERED (not a SELF-CENTERED) life?

Thursday
LIVING IN THE LIGHT OF THE LORD'S RETURN
Titus 2:13-14

Looking for that blessed hope, and the glorious appearing of the great God and our Saviour Jesus Christ; Who gave Himself for us, that He might redeem us from all iniquity, and purify unto Himself a peculiar people, zealous of good works.

We live in between times, suspended between the "already" and the "not yet." *Christ has appeared* and *will appear.* We are to look back on the one (Christ's first appearing and His grace) and forward to the other (His second appearing and His glory). Are you ready for the Lord to return? Today?

1. **Looking for**: Our *focus, gaze, attention, and thinking* should always include the return of the Lord. We should constantly live in the light of the Lord's return. The word translated **looking for** has the idea of *waiting with patience and confidence.* It is not hoping as if it might not happen, but a certain, eager, enthusiastic expectation. Do you remember your excitement as a small child as you **looked forward** to Christmas? Is there something you are now **looking forward** to? Summer vacation? Graduation? Marriage? With that same anticipation and excitement, **look for** the Lord to come back. Briefly explain how the following verses encourage us to **look for** our Lord to return for us.

• Philippians 3:20-21 _____

_____

• 2 Timothy 4:8 _____

_____

• 2 Peter 3:12-14 _____

_____

2. **That blessed hope**: The word **blessed** is used fifty times in the New Testament with the idea of *being fortunate, joyful, and happy.* **Hope** is *the happy anticipation of good,* not the fearful "I hope so—maybe—it could be—we'll just have to wait and see" type of **hope**. How should the confident expectation of the Lord's return effect our witnessing? _____

_____

How can the knowledge that the Lord could return any day, any hour, any minute, any second help us to say "no" to sin and temptation? _____

_____

Do you truly **hope** that the Lord would return today? _____

3. **And the glorious appearing of the great God and our Saviour Jesus Christ**: Christ's first **appearing** was a humble birth surrounded by animals, shepherds, hay, and straw. His second **appearing** will be with trumpets, shouts, angels, and glory. The word **glorious** is a glorious word. If you painted the word you would need to use colors as bright as fire. An attempt to describe the word leaves you short even if you use words like *honor, dignity, and praiseworthiness.* The Greek word is *doxa* from where we get our word doxology. If you can, write out the words to the Doxology that is found on the front or back covers of many hymnals today.

THE DOXOLOGY

_____

_____

_____

Read Matthew 25:31, Acts 1:11, 1 Thessalonians 4:13-18, 2 Peter 3:10, and Revelation 1:7 and explain what the return of the Lord may be like. _____

_____

_____

_____

4. Who gave Himself for us, that He might redeem us from all iniquity, and purify unto Himself a peculiar people, zealous of good works: Here Paul is using Old Testament words and terminology that we are not accustomed to, but his audience knew. Studying background, environment, and culture helps us to communicate the Gospel message in a way that makes sense.

- **Who gave Himself**—The Passover sacrifice
- **Redeem**—The Exodus: Israel's redemption from Egyptian bondage
- **A peculiar people**—A covenant made at Mt. Sinai where Israel became Jehovah's treasured possession

We can learn a great lesson from Paul's communication. Do you know the Gospel well enough to explain it to a 15-year-old street kid who never read the Bible before? _____

Could you put Christ's death, burial, and resurrection in plain words so that a 6-year-old child could understand? _____

Can you clearly explain how you know you are saved to one of your friends?_____

_____

From the list of references below, which would you use to explain each phrase? Write the reference in the blank.

Revelation 3:19	1 Peter 2:9-10	John 3:16	Ephesians 1:5-7

_____ • who gave Himself for us

_____ • that He might redeem us from all iniquity

_____ • and purify unto Himself a peculiar people

_____ • zealous of good works

There are too few **zealous** Christians in our churches and youth groups today who eagerly and enthusiastically seek to do good. How many Christian teens do you know who are hot, fervent, and on fire for God? _____

Are you one?_____

What did you learn from Titus 2:13-14 that will help you to eagerly and enthusiastically live for God (CHRIST-CENTERED, not SELF-CENTERED) as you look forward to His return?

Friday

LET NO MAN DESPISE YOU
Titus 2:15

These things speak, and exhort, and rebuke with all authority. Let no man despise thee.

It is not easy being a spiritual leader. Everything is great until you have to confront or admonish someone, and then, all of a sudden, you are the bad guy. We cannot help anyone by being easy on them. It takes a true leader who has both a heart for God and a heart for others to lovingly **rebuke** a friend who is starting to make self-centered choices. In today's study, Paul encouraged Titus to **authoritatively speak** the truth. Titus was to continue to **exhort** and to **rebuke** even if those he dealt with got upset with him, looked down on him, or even hated him.

1. **These things speak**: What **things** are Paul talking about? Basically, it refers *to everything that God had given Paul to give to Titus.* One commentator wrote to preachers, "Your words are not a bundle of hints and suggestions that might be helpful, but the Word of the Lord to the people." [5] Do you find it easy to question and disagree with what your pastor teaches? _____

_____

Someday God may want to use you as a pastor or a Sunday school teacher. Many teachers and preachers shoot their **authority** in the foot as they teach opinions and preferences as Bible convictions. It is great to have strong convictions as long as we do not put words into God's mouth and say He said something that He did not say. Why do you think a disciplined, intense, time-consuming study of God's Word is essential for all teachers and preachers? _____

_____

2. **Exhort**: This is a great word. It has *the idea of comforting, coming near or alongside of.* The type of leader who strives to stay on higher ground puts himself in a place where he can encourage others to join him. If you want to help others with their anger problems, what do you have to have under control in your own life? _____

In order to encourage someone struggling with a wicked thought life, what kind of thought life do you need to have?_____

To encourage your friends to take a stand against sin, what do you need to do in your own life?

_____

_____

Exhortation is *encouraging others to do right both by what you say and by what you do.* What did Paul *exhort* in 1 Timothy 2:1? _____

Titus was told to *exhort* who and what in Titus 1:9, 2:6, and 2:9? _____

3. *Rebuke: Exhortation* is **the positive approach of encouraging people to do what is right.** *Rebuking* or reproving is **the negative approach of convincing and correcting someone who does not admit there is a problem.** When was the last time you were personally **rebuked** for something? _____

Did you deserve it? _____

Did you enjoy it?_____

Learning to rightly receive **rebuke** is a lesson we all need to learn. It is amazing how defensive and self-centered we get when someone tries to tell us that we are wrong. Explain what each of the verses on the next page teach about rightly receiving **rebuke**.

- Proverbs 1:24-27 _____
- Proverbs 9:8 _____
- Proverbs 12:1 _____
- Proverbs 13:1 _____
- Proverbs 15:31-32 _____
- Proverbs 27:5 _____

4. **With all authority**: We cannot demand respect, but we can command respect. Titus had to stand in the face of argumentative teachers, older believers, and opinionated young men wondering why he should expect these guys to listen to him. If someday God puts you in the place of spiritual leadership, you will have to follow Titus' example to gain respect as a leader. A leader's ultimate goal is to get believers to hear, understand, apply, and obey God's Word. He does this in three ways: (1) **speaking** only God's Truth, (2) **exhorting** with God's Truth only, and (3) **rebuking** with God's Truth only. If it's not in the Bible, there is no **authority** and we should not act like there is! Where did Jesus say His teaching came from in John 7:16-17?_____

Jesus limited His teaching to only that which His Father gave Him. What did Jesus say about His teaching in John 8:28? _____

_____

What did Paul tell Timothy to preach in 2 Timothy 4:2? _____

_____

God's Word is our sufficient and supreme **authority**.

5. **Let no man despise you**: No one loves to be disliked, **despised,** or ignored. No one! The word **despise** has more of *the idea of ignoring, overlooking, or viewing as nothing* than it does to hate. With this definition in mind, explain what Hebrews 12:2 means when it says that Jesus, **for the joy that was set before Him, endured the cross, despising the shame**._____

_____

_____

Spiritual leaders can gain and keep the respect of others by simply living by our text, **These things speak, and exhort, and rebuke with all authority**. In other words,

> Teach and preach only Bible...Teach in a way that encourages people
> Lovingly confront when necessary...Speak with sincerity and integrity

What does Titus 2:15 teach that will help you have an impact on others, keep you from being ignored, and encourage you to live a CHRIST-CENTERED (not a SELF-CENTERED) life?

SATURDAY REVIEW
Titus 2:9-11

What have you learned from Titus 2:9-10 that helps you to be a hard-working, loyal employee who is known for living a CHRIST-CENTERED (not a SELF-CENTERED) life?

What did you learn from Titus 2:11 about our wonderful gift of salvation that keeps your focus on living a CHRIST-CENTERED (not a SELF-CENTERED) life?

SUNDAY REVIEW
Titus 2:12-15

How has Titus 2:12 impacted your life and helped you to say "no" to sin and "yes" to God as you seek to live a CHRIST-CENTERED (not a SELF-CENTERED) life?

What did you learn from Titus 2:13-14 that will help you to eagerly and enthusiastically live for God (CHRIST-CENTERED, not SELF-CENTERED) as you look forward to His return?

What does Titus 2:15 teach that will help you have an impact on others, keep you from being ignored, and encourage you to live a CHRIST-CENTERED (not a SELF-CENTERED) life?

55

Monday

REMEMBER OUR PUBLIC OBLIGATION TO UNBELIEVERS.
Titus 3:1-2

....

Put them in mind to be subject to principalities and powers, to obey magistrates, to be ready to every good work, To speak evil of no man, to be no brawlers, but gentle, shewing all meekness unto all men.

....

These two verses list seven responsibilities Christians must adhere to as they live face-to-face with unbelievers. We are constantly being watched to see if we believe what we say we do! As unbelievers examine your life, will they find a CHRIST-CENTERED or a self-centered lifestyle? _____

1. **Put them in mind**: Forgetting can be as humorous as it is horrible. We've all heard someone say, "You'd forget your head if it wasn't fastened on!" We forget what what we were going to say, what we were supposed to do, where we parked the car, and people's names. When was the last time you forgot something really important? (Or can you not remember?)_____

_____

Forgetting is quite frustrating, and even sad at times. Those suffering with Alzheimer's experience the pain of forgetting. They can't help it. But there are some who have chosen to be afflicted with "Spiritual Amnesia" and have actually forgotten about God and what He has done for them. What does 2 Peter 1:9 say about *forgetting*?_____

_____

What sad account does Judges 8:34 describe? _____

_____

Do you remember your God in prayer and devotions each day? _____

2. **Be subject to principalities and powers**: We are to submit to, or willingly place ourselves under the authority of, all government rulers and authorities. List the positions of two government **powers** or authorities. _____

_____

Give the names of two official **principalities** or rulers who live in your area. _____

_____

1 Peter 2:11-15 clearly explains our God-given responsibility towards police, judges, and other government officials. Briefly explain what these verses teach and why. _____

_____

3. **Obey magistrates**: The Greek word for this phrase is a combination of two words, one meaning to *agree* and the other describing someone who has *first place*. True **obedience** is *recognizing that we are not "number one" in this world and being willing to agree and submit to those who are "numero uno" in our lives.* How should this principle affect our relationship with employers, policemen, congressmen, the President, and even parents?_____

Do you personally struggle with submitting to authority? _____

How can consistent **obedience** help our opportunities to witness of our Lord?_____

_____

4. **Be ready to every good work**: Doing **good** beats doing nothing. Community service can open all kinds of doors for a verbal witness for Christ. People who do nothing and live by an "it's not my job" philosophy of life are bound to be bored (and boring) people. We must be prepared to help in every way we can.

What are some ways to get involved in the community you live? _____

_____

We can **work** together with government leaders as long as it is **good** and not evil they are involved in. The state has the power to punish evil and promote *good,* and we can cooperate as long as they do not get things turned around and promote evil instead of punishing it and oppose **good** instead of encouraging it. What are some popular social issues the world proposes and the Bible opposes? _____

_____

5. **Speak evil of no man**: We do not want to make enemies of those God has called us to witness to even if they are selfishly wicked. We must be careful to attack the sin we hate and not the sinner. According to 1 Timothy 2:1-3, what did Paul tell Timothy he should do for those in authority and why? _____

_____

_____

The Greek word for **speak evil** literally means *to defame, to revile, to rail on, or to show contempt for.* Sometimes unbelievers **speak evil** of Christians. According to 1 Peter 4:4, why is this? _____

_____

6. **Be no brawlers**: Don't fight! Don't pick fights! What does the foolish man of Proverbs 18:6 call for?

_____

According to Proverbs 13:10, contention is always a result of what? _____

Don't be known as a contentious fighter.

7. **But gentle**: Warren Wiersbe calls **gentleness** *"a sweet reasonableness."* [6] It has *the spirit of consideration and seeks to be fair in dealing with others.* What does 2 Timothy 2:24 say about fighting and gentleness? _____

_____

8. **Shewing all meekness unto all men**: What does 2 Timothy 2:25-26 teach could be the result of a **meek**, kind, caring spirit? _____

_____

Which of these seven responsibilities from Titus 3:1-2 do you do well on?
Which of these seven responsibilities do you need to work on?
What needs to change to help you be more CHRIST-CENTERED and less SELF-CENTERED?

Tuesday
REMEMBER OUR PAST SINFULNESS.
Titus 3:3

For we ourselves also were sometimes foolish, disobedient, deceived, serving divers lusts and pleasures, living in malice and envy, hateful, and hating one another.

We must be careful not to be too hard or critical on unbelievers. Remembering what we were before God saved and changed us should help us to be more understanding towards those who do not know Christ. Titus 3:3 lists seven characteristics of an unbeliever which, sadly to say, are also seen in the hearts of many self-centered believers.

1. **For we ourselves also were sometimes foolish: Foolishness** is not only bound in the heart of a child, but in teens and adults as well. Let's never forget what we were and be thankful for what God is helping us to become. The word **foolish** comes from two words, one meaning *not* and the other *to exercise the mind*. **Foolishness** often is a choice. If we do not study God's Word to gain His wisdom, we will continue to live and act like fools. List some of the marks of a **fool** from the Proverbs passages below. Hopefully, this does not describe you.

- Proverbs 1:7
- Proverbs 10:1
- Proverbs 14:8
- Proverbs 14:16
- Proverbs 18:6
- Proverbs 26:11
- Proverbs 1:22
- Proverbs 12:16
- Proverbs 17:10
- Proverbs 20:3

2. **Disobedient: Disobedience** has the idea of *being unpersuadable, disagreeable, and unfriendly.* A **disobedient** child rebels and refuses to agree with his parents' authority. How do we sometimes act like rebellious, **disobedient** children in our relationship with God? _____

_____

God gives three passages of Scripture that teach little kids how to obey their parents quickly, sweetly, and completely. Read Ephesians 6:1, Ephesians 6:2, and Colossians 3:20. Which verse goes with which aspect of obedience listed below?

Quickly: _____ **Sweetly:** _____ **Completely:** _____

How well do you obey God with these three principles in mind? _____

_____

3. **Deceived**: Personal deception can be very dangerous. When we choose to be disobedient to God we often take the next step and *disagree with God.* Why does God warn us to be not **deceived** in 1 Corinthians 15:33?_____

How about in Galatians 6:7?_____

What does 2 John 7 say that true **deceivers** refuse to believe? _____

_____

Before we acknowledged that Jesus Christ is the Son of God and the only way of salvation and forgiveness of sins, we too were *deceived.* Take a minute and personally thank the Lord for the Truth that can set us free from deception.

4. **Serving divers lusts and pleasures**: Slavery did not end at the end of the Civil War. Unbelievers are in constant bondage to sin and its penalty. What is called liberty or freedom to sin is actually bondage to **lust** and desire. True freedom comes from the grace of God which gives us the strength to say "no" to sin.

Name three sins that you think would be easy to become addicted to. _____

_____

_____

5. **Living in malice**: How would you define **malice**? _____

_____

The Greek word for **malice** simply means *bad, evil, wicked, or depraved.* Those who live in **malice** are spending their time in sin. They are living their lives in wickedness. Who do you know that lives in outright sin and does not care what God or anyone else thinks? _____

_____

What do you think goes through their minds when they think of eternity and standing before God?

_____

Do you spend more time "doing good" or **living in malice**?_____

6. **Living in envy**: **Envy** is *wanting something that is not yours to have.* **Envy** is never satisfied. **Envy** craves more and more. Wanting what others have and wanting them not to have it is the essence of true *envy.* Who are you jealous or **envious** of? _____

_____

What do you want that God has not already given you? _____

_____

Are you thankful for what you do have or do you want more? _____

_____

7. **Hateful, and hating one another**: We live in a world of **hate**! **Hatred** is one of the most self-centered sins known to man. We are commanded to salute one another, greet one another, be kind to one another, bear one another's burdens, pray for one another, serve one another, submit to one another, esteem one another, comfort one another, consider one another, and love one another—not **hate one another***!* Is there anyone on earth you **hate** and refuse to forgive? _____

_____

How should Christ's teaching in Matthew 22:37-39 impact a **hateful** person? _____

_____

_____

The more self-centered we are, the more we will **hate**. The more CHRIST-CENTERED we are, the more we will love.

> List some of the characteristics of a SELF-CENTERED unbeliever
> mentioned in Titus 3:3 that you are thankful God saved you from.

Wednesday
Remember our present salvation.
Titus 3:4-5

....

But after that the kindness and love of God our Saviour toward man appeared, Not by works of righteousness which we have done, but according to His mercy He saved us, by the washing of regeneration, and renewing of the Holy Ghost.

....

Yesterday we were reminded of what we were or could have been if we had never been *saved* by the grace of God. Today and tomorrow we are going to meditate on our undeserved salvation. It is amazing that when words like God, salvation, Jesus, or Saviour enter a conversation, people either get embarrassed, angry, or quiet. Satan does not want us to talk about, or even think about, his defeat and our eternal victory accomplished by the death, burial, and resurrection of Jesus Christ! Are you thankful you're saved? Take a minute and tell God how thankful you really are.

"HE SAVED US!"

1. The key phrase of these verses is **He saved us**. When and where did God **save** you? _____

_____

_____

Surrounding these three words are statements of what God has graciously done for us. We are saved because of **God's kindness, God's love, God's mercy, God's washing of regeneration, God's renewing by the Holy Spirit, God's Son, Jesus Christ our Saviour, and God's grace.** Today we want to take some time to thank **God, our Saviour,** for each of these incredible gifts to us.

2. **Thank God for His *kindness.*** God's *genuine concern, generosity, and goodness is seen in what He did for undeserving sinners like you and me.* Ephesians 2:4-7 wraps God's **kindness** in **love**, **mercy**, and grace. Read Ephesians 2:4-7 and write out verse seven. _____

_____

_____

What does Ephesians 4:32 teach us we should learn from God's **kindness**? _____

_____

Our **kindness** to others is a great indicator that we understand God's **kindness** to us. Take some time in prayer and thank God for His **kindness** to you.

3. **Thank God for His *love.*** God's **love** for us is more than good feelings and emotions. The word used for **love** in this verse combines two words, one meaning to *have affection for* and the other meaning *man*. This **love** is the highest form of compassion which looks for ways to help those who are suffering or in danger or pain. What does Lamentations 3:22 teach about God's compassion for us? _____

_____

What similar phrase is found in Psalm 86:15, Psalm 111:4, and Psalm 145:8?_____

_____

_____

Take some time in prayer right now and thank God for His compassionate **love**.

4. **Thank God for His *mercy*.** One commentator wrote, "We did not deserve deliverance from sin and death. We did not deserve to be born again, recreated in the very image of our Lord. We did not deserve to become God's children and joint-heirs with His only begotten Son, Jesus Christ. We did not deserve the promise of everlasting life, which we will spend in heaven in the continual presence of God."[7] Because of our sin, what do we deserve? _____

_____

God is not fickle or moody about His **mercy**. It is forever. Read Psalm 136:1-26 and list the number of times God uses the phrase: His **mercy** endureth forever._____

Take some time in prayer and thank God for His **mercy** to such an undeserving sinner as yourself.

5. **Thank God for His *washing of regeneration*.** If we seriously study our own hearts we would never say that we are innately good, but would admit that we are filthy, dirty, rotten sinners. **Regeneration** is the Bible word for *being born again or receiving new life*. It is more than turning over a new leaf; it is *a brand-new life from which the old has been forgiven and treated as if it never existed*. When you accepted Christ as your personal Saviour, how many of your sins were forgiven? _____

At that point of salvation, a brand-new life started. Isn't it amazing that God would do that for us?

_____

Take some time in prayer and thank God for **washing** and cleansing you from your past sin and **regenerating** you by giving you a brand-new life.

6. **Thank God for His *renewing by the Holy Spirit*.** Upon salvation the Holy Spirit indwelt you and began changing you. According to 2 Corinthians 5:17, what does God want to do to us by His Spirit? _____

_____

Ephesians 1:13-14 teaches that the Holy Spirit gives spiritual life, sustains spiritual life, empowers spiritual life, and guarantees that our spiritual life will become eternal life. Why? Because He is the seal, or guarantee, of eternal life. Take some time in prayer and thank God for the indwelling of His comforting, empowering Holy Spirit.

7. The bottom line of what we learned from Titus 3:4-5 is _____

_____

_____

"HE SAVED US!"

Think through each of the five aspects of salvation listed in
Titus 3:4-5 and again thank God for His great salvation.

Thursday
Remember our future position in Christ.
Titus 3:6-7

....

Which He shed on us abundantly through Jesus Christ our Saviour; That being justified by His grace, we should be made heirs according to the hope of eternal life.

....

Let's continue from yesterday thanking God for our great salvation. We will learn a few more truths that we can combine with the five from Titus 3:4-5. We will see that we are not just saved from the penalty of sin and the power of sin, but also from the presence of sin as we live for **eternity** with God.

1. **Thank God for *Jesus Christ our Saviour.*** Jesus became man. Jesus lived a sinless life. Jesus was mocked. Jesus was scourged. Jesus was crucified. Jesus died! Jesus was buried! Jesus rose from the grave! List three other religious leaders who have lived, died, and are still dead. _____

_____

What word in 1 John 2:2 and 1 John 4:10 means that Jesus took our place by paying the price for our sin? _____

What Jesus did, no other man could do. What did the angels call Christ in Luke 2:11? _____

_____

What did the Samaritans call Jesus in John 4:42? _____

What did Paul call our Lord Jesus Christ in Philippians 3:20? _____

What did Peter call our Lord Jesus Christ in 2 Peter 1:11? _____

What did John say God the Father sent His Son to be in 1 John 4:14? _____

_____

Take some time in prayer right now and thank God for sending His Son to be your **Saviour** by saving you from the penalty, power, and presence of sin.

2. **Thank God for *His justification.*** Romans 5:1 clearly says, Therefore being **justified** by faith, we have peace with God through our Lord Jesus Christ. **Justification** is *that legal aspect of our salvation whereby we are treated as if we never sinned.* Our past sins are forgiven. What an incredible blessing! From Romans 3:24-25 and Galatians 2:16, write a few short statements explaining **justification**.

_____

_____

_____

_____

_____

3. **Thank God for *His grace.*** "Amazing *grace*, how sweet the sound." *Grace* is *the undeserved favor God shows toward us.* It is not really easy to explain or define, but by *God's* **grace** we are saved. What did Paul tell Titus about **grace** in Titus 2:11? _____

Read 2 Timothy 1:9-10. God did not save us according to our own works, but according to what?

_____

How many times is **grace** mentioned in Ephesians 2:4-9? _____

What two principles can you learn about **grace** from the Ephesians passage? _____

_____

How old were you when you received God's **grace** and were saved? _____

Take some time and thank God in prayer for His amazing **grace**.

4. **Thank God that *He made us heirs.*** Knowing our own hearts, we are the first to admit we do not deserve God's salvation. Not only did He save us, He made us **heirs** for eternity. How did James describe the **heirs** in James 2:5?_____

_____

Paul tells us in Romans 8:16 that the Holy Spirit gives us an internal assurance that we are God's children. Since God assures us of our salvation by His Spirit, what else does His Spirit assure us of in verse 17?

_____

Have you ever inherited something from a relative?_____

Are you in line to inherit something in the future?_____

If we never inherit anything here on earth, as Christians, we still have the joy of knowing that we have an inheritance in heaven that will far outshine anything we can ever get on earth. How does 1 Peter 1:4 describe our eternal inheritance?_____

_____

According to Ephesians 5:5, who will *not* receive an inheritance from God? _____

_____

Take some time and thank God for the privilege of being one of His **heirs**.

5. **Thank God for *the hope of eternal life.*** How long is **eternal**? _____

_____

What word does John 3:16 use in place of **eternal**?_____

This **hope** is a *full assurance and a happy anticipation of living forever with God in heaven*. Thank your Lord for **eternal** salvation! Take some time and thank God in prayer for **the hope of eternal life**.

> What did you learn from Titus 3:6-7 that fills your heart with joy and
> thanksgiving for God's amazing grace and incredible salvation?

Friday

REMEMBER OUR PRESENT RESPONSIBILITIES.
Titus 3:8

. . . .

This is a faithful saying, and these things I will that thou affirm constantly, that they which have believed in God might be careful to maintain good works. These things are good and profitable unto men.

. . . .

All good messages have an attention-grabbing introduction and a conclusion that passionately wraps up the purpose of the message in a concise, understandable statement. Paul uses Titus 3:8 to conclude the teaching of **these things** from chapter two and the first seven verses of chapter three. Today we will study each phrase of this conclusion to clearly understand its practical application.

1. **This is a faithful saying**: Have you ever been in a service when your mind begins to drift or wander and you were shocked back into reality when the speaker loudly says, "OK, listen up!" or "Hey, I need everyone's attention right up here!" What causes our minds to zone out so that even when we are looking straight ahead, eyes wide open and smiling, our minds are visiting some planet in outer space? List three things that could make it easy for us to let our minds wander during preaching. _____

_____

_____

There are a number of ways you could restate the phrase **this is a faithful saying**. "Here is a trustworthy statement." "You can take this one to the bank!" "Hey gang, sit up and take notice!" "I want you to look at me and listen to this!" Actually, we should look at every truth from God's Word as a **faithful saying** and work hard to listen, learn, and live like our Lord.

2. **And these things**: **These things** are the **things** that Paul has been putting an emphasis on in chapter two and the beginning of chapter three. Very briefly, explain what **things** were addressed to the various individuals in the churches on the island of Crete.

• The aged men (2:2) _____

_____

• The aged women (2:3)_____

_____

• The young women (2:4-5) _____

_____

• The young men (2:6-8)_____

_____

• The servants (2:9-10)_____

_____

• All believers looking for the Lord's return (2:11-15) _____

_____

• All believers living a Christ-centered life before unbelievers (3:1-7)_____

_____

3. **I will that thou affirm constantly**: Paul wanted Titus to **constantly** remind his friends in Crete of the impact of a godly life. Getting your friends to listen is a huge part of sharing the truth. Titus probably sounded like a sixth grade Sunday school teacher with phrases like, "Look in my eyes! Do I have your attention? Are you with me? Is everyone awake and listening?" What are some good ways to keep the attention of a young class so they can learn what God has for them? _____

_____

4. **That they which have believed in God**: Paul is writing to **believers**, those who have put their total trust and faith **in God**. What did God use in your life (parents, pastor, revival, camp, etc.) to cause you to trust or **believe in God**? _____

Have you ever let God use you to encourage your friends to put their trust **in God** by witnessing or inviting them to church or camp? _____

Read Acts 28:23-24. In this passage Paul persuaded men to **believe**. How long did he reason with the people who came to hear him?_____

What did he use to **persuade** them? _____

According to verse 24, how did they respond? _____

We may not win many, but we can be faithful, like Paul, to passionately persuade many to **believe in the true God**.

5. **Might be careful to maintain good works**: These words actually reveal our heart's desire behind what we do. The Greek word for **might be careful** deals *with feelings and emotions and has the idea of being anxious or "full of care."* The **maintaining of good works** should be an emotional, driving force in our lives. It is not just an academic view to be considered, but a life-changing principle to be lived. List five **good works** mentioned in chapter two that you struggle with and need to passionately work on.

_____

_____

On a scale from one to ten, rate your emotional, full-of-care, life-motivating desire to live a CHRIST-CENTERED life. _____

6. **These things are good and profitable unto men**: Those who work hard to do right can have a great impact on those around them. For some, it will introduce them to Jesus Christ and eternal salvation. For others, it will show them the wasteful, shallow, meaningless, unfulfilled, unsatisfying life that they live can be changed to a productive, deep, meaningful, fulfilling and satisfying life! How have you seen your CHRIST-CENTERED life **profit** others?_____

_____

How did Titus 3:8 touch your heart and motivate you to impact unbelievers by living a CHRIST-CENTERED (not a SELF-CENTERED) life?

SATURDAY REVIEW
Titus 3:1-3

Which of these seven responsibilities from Titus 3:1-2 do you do well on? Which of these seven responsibilities do you need to work on? What needs to change to help you be more CHRIST-CENTERED and less SELF-CENTERED?

List some of the characteristics of a SELF-CENTERED unbeliever mentioned in Titus 3:3 that you are thankful God saved you from.

SUNDAY REVIEW
Titus 3:4-8

Think through each of the five aspects of salvation listed in Titus 3:4-5 and again thank God for His great salvation.

What did you learn from Titus 3:6-7 that fills your heart with joy and thanksgiving for God's amazing grace and incredible salvation?

How did Titus 3:8 touch your heart and motivate you to impact unbelievers by living a CHRIST-CENTERED (not a SELF-CENTERED) life?

Monday

AVOID WORTHLESS, TIME-WASTING ARGUMENTS.
Titus 3:9

....

But avoid foolish questions, and genealogies, and contentions, and strivings about the law; for they are unprofitable and vain.

....

There are only so many hours in a day and only so many opportunities to help people know and understand the absolute truth of God's Word. It is easier to argue with other so-called believers than it is to witness to unbelievers. It is easier to quarrel than it is to be kind and considerate. It is easier to fight and cause division than it is to reach the people God has called you to serve. Paul encourages Titus to avoid and stay away from such time-wasting arguments and faithfully continue to teach and preach the truth.

1. **But avoid**: The word **avoid** simply means *to purposely turn away from.* Titus, the elders he appointed, and the Christians on the island of Crete were to purposely turn away from false teachers. These guys pretended to be spiritual by arguing about spiritual things but actually lived ungodly, self-centered lives which hindered the credibility of the Gospel. False teaching is incredibly destructive, whether it comes from an egomaniac's pulpit or from guys at high school who say the Bible is outdated and too old to affect our lives today. Match the following effects of false teaching by drawing a line to the correct references below.

1 Timothy 1:19	It troubles the soul.
1 Timothy 1:20	It shipwrecks faith.
Acts 15:24	It leads to blasphemy.
2 Timothy 2:14	It leads to spiritual ruin.
2 Timothy 2:16	It results in ungodliness.
2 Timothy 2:17	It spreads like gangrene.

2. **Foolish**: Paul mentions four areas of concern for Titus. All four concerns can easily waste a spiritual leader's time and distract him from what he is supposed to be doing. Pretend your mind is a thesaurus and list as many synonyms for the word **foolish** you can. (Here's a hint. The Greek word for **foolish** is *moros*!)

_____

3. **Foolish questions, and genealogies, and contentions, and strivings**: We have more important things to do than to sit around arguing about **questions** from the Bible that even the greatest theologians in history have not agreed on. Such discussions could be *nothing more than a way to avoid doing what we do know and understand.* What would be more beneficial: arguing about where Cain got his wife or memorizing the book of James? _____

Would it be better to spend all your time trying to get your friends to agree with your view of God's sovereignty or to share the Gospel with an unbeliever? _____

4. **Foolish questions**: Controversies that are based on speculations, opinions, and human reasoning, rather than God's Word, are **foolish**. List what 1 Timothy 6:4-5 says is the result of doting about **questions**? (By the way, the word **doting** refers to an unhealthy, morbid fascination.) _____

_____

5. **Foolish genealogies**: According to 1 Timothy 1:4, what does listening to endless **genealogies** result in?

_____

We do not gain favor with God by being "born right" as many, including Nicodemus in John 3, believed. If Nicodemus did believe that he was *born* into God's favor, what did Jesus tell him in John 3:3?

_____

The term "born again" shows that you were born once physically, and a second time spiritually. When were you *born again*? _____

6. **Foolish contentions**: The word **contention** implies *a quarrel or a wrangling* and is often translated *debate, strife, or variance.* **Contention** is often listed in the long list of sins that God hates. Read the following passages and summarize God's view of the listed sins which include strife or **contention**.

      Romans 1:28-32   Romans 13:13-14   1 Corinthians 3:1-6   Galatians 5:19-21

_____

_____

_____

7. **Foolish strivings about the law**: The word *striving* is simply *a nice way to say fighting*! According to James 4:1 and Proverbs 13:10, where do all fights or **foolish strivings** come from? _____

_____

How could selfishness, or self-centeredness, keep us wasting our precious time and keep us from doing what we should be doing?_____

_____

_____

8. **For they are unprofitable and vain**: The best way to apply this phrase is to read this testimony from Bible commentator Warren Wiersbe.

> "I recall being approached by a young man after a Bible lesson and getting involved with him in all sorts of hypothetical questions of doctrine. 'Now, if this were true...if that were true...' was about all he could say. I was very inexperienced at the time; I should have ignored him in a gracious way. As it was, I missed the opportunity to talk with several sincere people who had personal problems and wanted help. I have learned that professed Christians who like to argue about the Bible are usually covering up some sin in their lives, are very insecure, and are usually unhappy at work or at home." [8]

How has God used Titus 3:9 to help you avoid foolish, time-wasting arguments so you can concentrate on living a CHRIST-CENTERED (not a SELF-CENTERED) life?

Tuesday
DEALING WITH HERETICS
Titus 3:10-11

. . . .

A man that is an heretick after the first and second admonition reject; Knowing that he that is such is subverted, and sinneth, being condemned of himself.

. . . .

To paraphrase the verse above, Paul tells Titus to warn a divisive person once, and then warn him a **second** time. After that, have nothing to do with him. You may be sure that such a man is warped and sinful; he is self-condemned. I remember as a kid trying to visualize what a **heretic** (a hairy tick) looked like. I never did get a good look at one but now understand how important it is to discern what a real **heretic** looks like to know how to deal with them.

1. **A man that is an heretic**: A **heretic** is simply *a man, woman, or teenager who knows he or she is right and everybody else is wrong.* Paul describes these problem people in 2 Timothy 3:1-5. How many different words or phrases did Paul use in those verses to describe the characteristics of the false-teaching **heretics**?_____

Paul dealt with **heretics** in the first chapter of Titus. What three terms did Paul use to describe these **heretics** in Titus 1:10? _____

_____

According to the same verse, were there many or few? _____

Titus 1:11 tells what a **heretic** does, why he does it, and what must be done about it. From this verse, what does a **heretic** do? _____

Why does a **heretic** do what he does?_____

What should we as Christians and spiritual leaders do about it? _____

In verse 12, how did one of their own prophets describe the Cretian **heretics**? _____

_____

Both Titus 1:16 and 2 Timothy 3:5 show that these men were not rebellious and disobedient believers; they were not believers at all as proved by what they taught and how they lived. Write out both of those verses below.

Titus 1:16 _____

_____

_____

2 Timothy 3:5 _____

_____

_____

Do you know anyone who pretends to be spiritual but lives a wicked, ungodly, self-centered life?

_____

Should you be best friends with those kind of people? _____

From Titus 3:10 and 2 Timothy 3:5, what type of relationship should you have with them and what should you do if they want to argue and disagree with what you believe and how you live?

_____

2. **After the first and second admonition reject**: Most divisive people will not submit to the Word or to godly leaders in the church. They become their own law and are not concerned with truth or unity. Christians are to take a stand against false teaching and be Bible-based separatists but are not to swing the ax too harshly or too quickly. There are times to separate and times not to separate. When the purity of the Gospel is attacked, there is no question; we must separate. On other issues that fall into the categories of preferences and opinions, we have to ask God for wisdom and be very careful. How many times should you approach a false-teaching, divisive **heretic** according to Titus 3:10? _____

God is a forgiving God who gives *second* chances...and so should we. According to Titus 1:13, what is your goal in approaching them twice with the truth? _____

_____

Instead of immediately giving up on these **heretics**, do everything you can to get them to understand the truth. Be careful not to join in with them or agree with what they say, but try to help them by using God's Word. How would you help someone who believed they had to be baptized in order to be saved and go to heaven? _____

_____

What would you say to those who believe there are many different ways to get to God other than through Jesus Christ? _____

_____

Did you give Scripture references for those last two answers? If you did, great; if you did not, remember it is not what *we* have to say but what *God* has already said in His Word that is the truth.

3. **Knowing that he that is such is subverted, and sinneth, being condemned of himself**: These self-centered **heretics** are perverted and warped. The word for **subverted** means *to turn inside out*. A literal translation of this phrase says that such a man is warped in character, keeps on sinning, and has **condemned himself**. He is warped, **sinful**, knows it, but doesn't care! Some want money, some want popularity, some want power. How is this kind of leader different than the CHRIST-CENTERED leader we are supposed to be? _____

_____

What did God teach you today from Titus 3:10-11 about dealing with
SELF-CENTERED heretics who oppose a CHRIST-CENTERED life and ministry?

Wednesday
TITUS, A GOOD GUY TO HAVE AROUND
Titus 3:12

....

When I shall send Artemas unto thee, or Tychicus, be diligent to come unto me to Nicopolis: for I have determined there to winter.

....

There are some people you just love to hang out with, and others you can't wait to get away from. Titus was one of those guys who had a great attitude towards life and you'd just love to have around. There was no doubt that Titus had the testimony of being CHRIST-CENTERED and not self-centered. Paul was encouraging Titus to make his plans to join him for the **winter** and much of what we know about Titus' life and character is from Paul's letters to the church at Corinth. Today we will study the life of Titus, the kind of guy you'd just love to have around.

1. **When I shall send Artemas unto thee, or Tychicus**: Paul needed Titus and sent one or two qualified leaders to take his place on the island of Crete. We do not know too much about Art and Ty but do know that Paul trusted them to carry on the spiritual leadership of the Cretian churches. If Paul was looking today for a couple of qualified, CHRIST-CENTERED leaders, would he choose you? _____

_____

Why or why not? _____

Who do you know that has the testimony and leadership ability to step in at a moment's notice and help their friends with their spiritual needs? _____

Continue to grow and change and you can be one of those individuals.

2. **Be diligent to come unto me to Nicopolis: for I have determined there to winter**: Paul wanted Titus to leave Crete and join him for the **winter**. Not only could Paul spend some time mentoring Titus as he did Timothy, but Titus was one of those guys who was a comfort and a joy to have around. Below is a list of things we know about Titus from other portions of Scripture.

- Titus was a comfort in tough situations.
- Titus knew how to help handle difficult problems.
- Titus had a joyful, refreshing attitude about life.
- Titus loved people; it was not put on or fake, but from the heart.
- Titus was not in it for himself (money, popularity, power, prestige); his heart was for others...and everybody knew it.
- Titus was one of those guys you'd just love having around.

3. **Titus was a comfort in tough situations.** Read 2 Corinthians 7:5-7. What four problems did Paul face according to verse 5? _____

_____

_____

What did God do to comfort Paul and those with him according to 2 Corinthians 7:6?

_____

According to 2 Corinthians 7:7, how did Titus comfort and encourage Paul?_____

_____

4. **Titus knew how to help handle difficult problems.** In the space below, write out 2 Corinthians 2:13.

_____

_____

Paul left Troas to find Titus. He was so troubled by the stuff going on in Corinth that he needed to talk to Titus to see what they were going to do to work these things out. When you face difficult problems, who do you go to? _____

Does anyone come to you for help when they are in trouble? _____

What does 2 Corinthians 1:4 say about comforting others? _____

_____

5. **Titus had a joyful, refreshing attitude about life.** Titus obviously was known for his joy according to 2 Corinthians 7:13-14. Joyful people are fun to be around. Are you known for your moodiness or for your joyful spirit? _____

Our relationship with God, both in salvation and in sanctification, is the basis of true joy. Read Isaiah 12 and thank God for His salvation.

6. **Titus loved people; it was not put on or fake, but from the heart.** How did Paul describe Titus' love for the people in 2 Corinthians 7:15-16?_____

_____

What was Paul thankful to God for in 2 Corinthians 8:16?_____

Our love for God and others is a great way to turn people's attention toward God. What did Jesus tell His disciples in John 13:35 when they asked Him how people will know that they were His disciples?_____

_____

Are you known for being loving and kind? _____

How could you improve in this area? _____

7. **Titus was not in it for himself (money, popularity, power, prestige); his heart was for others...and everybody knew it.** Titus knew how to live a Christ-centered life in a self-centered world. How does 2 Corinthians 12:18-19 describe his unselfishness? _____

_____

8. **Titus was one of those guys you'd just love having around.** Because of his joy, his love, his comfort, his wisdom, and his encouraging spirit, Titus was great to have around. Could the same be said about you?

_____

Titus lived a CHRIST-CENTERED life. What did you learn from Titus 3:12 that will help you to be like Titus, a guy people loved to have around?

Thursday
TAKE CARE OF GOD'S SERVANTS.
Titus 3:13-14

Bring Zenas the lawyer and Apollos on their journey diligently, that nothing be wanting unto them. And let our's also learn to maintain good works for necessary uses, that they be not unfruitful.

A few verses back Paul spent time condemning false teachers and now he commends those who teach the truth. Paul had asked Titus for two favors: one was to visit him in Nicopolis and the other was to help two faithful leaders get everything they need together for what seemed to be a mission trip.

1. **Zenas the lawyer**: All we know about **Zenas** was that he was a **lawyer**. Either he knew the laws of the land or was an expert in Jewish law. Either way, all we know is that he was highly respected by Paul who was sending him on a special mission. There are many true, faithful servants in our Christian family that we will never hear or know about, but they are loved and accepted by God for their faithful service. How important is it to be well-known and highly respected by others? _____

_____

Some of the greatest servants of God we have never read or heard about. How does Colossians 3:23-24 apply to this principle of life? _____

_____

Be committed to pleasing God and God alone. It does not matter how many people of the world think we are doing well, as long as we hear our Lord say "well done" when we stand before Him someday.

2. **Apollos**: **Apollos** was a bit more well-known than his partner **Zenas**. We first hear of him in Acts 18:24-28 where a godly couple, Aquilla and Priscilla, sought to help him understand more clearly the Gospel of Jesus Christ. How does Acts 18:24-26 describe **Apollos** and his ministry? _____

_____

Some enjoyed **Apollos'** teaching so much they actually became a bit divisive in the church, following a man instead of the simple teaching of the Gospel. According to 1 Corinthians 1:11-12, what three men were the early believers guilty of following? _____

_____

Technically, there are not great men of God but only a great God of men. What are the dangers of getting our eyes focused on a man and not focused on God? _____

_____

3. **Bring [them] on their journey diligently**: Paul was asking Titus to help his friends get ready for a trip they had to take. The interesting word in this phrase is the word **diligently**. **Diligence** is *a necessary character quality found in godly leaders*. **Diligence** is *looking at each task I am given as a special assignment from the Lord and using all the talents and energies I have to accomplish it*. Read Romans 12:11 and Colossians 3:23. Would you consider yourself a **diligent** servant of God? _____

4. **That nothing be wanting unto them**: Paul asked Titus to help **Zenas and Apollos** get **on their journey** and to make sure that they had everything they needed. The word **wanting** actually does not refer to what is wanted but *what is needed*. Some people have more needs than others. Most of us have very few needs but many wants. Fill in the blanks from Philippians 4:19.

But my _____ shall supply all your _____ according to His _____ in glory by Christ Jesus.

What does Matthew 6:8 say about our needs being known by God? _____

_____

Take some time and meditate on Matthew 6:24-34. God knows our needs and will take care of us. What two examples does God use in Matthew 6 to remind us that He will take care of us? _____

_____

5. **And let our's also learn to maintain good works for necessary uses**: Paul reminds Titus of the main theme of the letter which was to insist that the Cretian believers **maintain good works**. The theme of doing **good** is like a thread running all through Paul's letter to Titus. In chapter one an elder was someone who loves what is _____

Paul said in Titus 1:16 the false teachers were unfit for doing anything_____

The older women in Titus 2:3 were to teach what is _____

We are told in Titus 2:7 that Titus himself was to be an example to the young men by doing what is ____

_____

We read in Titus 2:14 that our redemption in Christ should motivate us to be a people eager to do what is _____

We are told in Titus 3:1 that our attitude towards all authority should make us ready to do whatever is

_____

Titus 3:8 shows us that those who have trusted in God may be careful to devote themselves to do what is _____

And that brings us to our study today in Titus 3:14 where we are encouraged to maintain _____ works. God wants us to be _____

6. **That they be not unfruitful**: Paul ends his letter with the picture of fruitfulness. A self-centered Christian cannot be fruitful; a Christ-centered Christian can be fruitful. What do you have in your spiritual fruit basket? _____

_____

_____

> How have the principles of Titus 3:13-14 encouraged you to be a CHRIST-CENTERED,
> fruitful believer who loves to do good, rather than a SELF-CENTERED,
> unfruitful believer who seldom does good?

Friday
So long! Adios! Au revoir!
Titus 3:15

....

All that are with me salute thee. Greet them that love us in the faith. Grace be with you all. Amen.

....

Often "good-byes" are not much fun but are filled with tears and wishful thinking that things did not have to change. "Good-byes" are a part of life. Some say "good-bye" and others say "good riddance!" It usually depends on the impact you have had on those you are saying "good-bye" to and the legacy you leave for them to remember. When you say "good-bye," what do those you leave remember about you?

1. **All that are with me**: Friends are great. Everyone likes to be liked and loves to be loved. Paul had companions and friends that served with him and encouraged him in his ministry. List the names of your three best friends. _____

Do your best friends have a heart for God and encourage you to serve Him? _____

How did David describe his friends in Psalm 119:63? _____

What did Solomon say about companions or friends in Proverbs 13:20 and 28:7? _____

_____

Your friends will either help or hinder your relationship with God. According to Ecclesiastes 4:9-10, how can a godly friend help you when you feel like giving up?_____

_____

To have the right kind of friends, we must be the right kind of friend. Who have you been a spiritual encouragement to in the last month? _____

2. **Salute thee**: You can almost see Paul's friends lining up before Titus in a military fashion, with outstretched fingers to their foreheads yelling, "Yes, Sir, Sergeant Titus, Sir!" Actually, the word **salute** has the idea of *wishing you well with the desire to be affectionately remembered*. This greeting seemed to have taken various forms in the early church. How did individuals **salute** according to Romans 16:16 and 2 Corinthians 13:12?_____

How did Paul **greet** the disciples in Acts 20:1? _____

How did John encourage his readers to **greet** each other in 3 John 14? _____

_____

Various cultures **greet** each other in various ways. There is a South American hug or *abrazo*. Middle Eastern custom uses a type of ceremonial kiss. I understand that Eskimos rub noses. Most of us in America shake hands, give a high five, or simply say, "Hey!" The type of greeting is not the issue here, but rather the obvious condition of the heart and the expression of **love** for each other. It's pretty tough to hug someone you hate or give a high five to someone you cannot stand. Is there anyone on this earth that you cannot stand and you need to ask God to give you a heart of **love** for? _____

_____

If so, spend some time with the Lord right now and ask Him to help you change.

3. **Greet them that love us in the faith**: Paul is referring to those who have a true, genuine, CHRIST-CENTERED **love** for each other. This is not talking about those who have personalities that click or have a lot in common, but of *a Christian bond that is cemented together by the Holy Spirit of God*. One of

76

the best verses that describe this kind of **love** is 1 Timothy 1:5. According to that verse, **love** is motivated from what three sources? _____

_____

What is unfeigned **faith**? _____

How does someone with a fake **love** act around you? _____

_____

Now describe a friend who has genuine **love** and concern. _____

_____

How does Peter encourage us to **love** other Christians in 1 Peter 1:22? _____

_____

4. **Grace be with you all**: Paul could have said it this way, "May God's divine favor and blessing stay **with you** and comfort everyone of **you**." I have heard some say that the Apostle Paul must have been from the South because he used the words **you all**. I don't remember seeing North Carolina in the list of places in Paul's missionary journeys, but I do know that he had a genuine desire that all believers would enjoy and benefit from the **grace** of God. In Acts 11:23, what was Barnabas' response when he saw the **grace** of God? _____

According to Romans 5:15, do we have to earn or work for **grace**? _____

Paul said in 1 Corinthians 15:10 that his character, his accomplishments, and all his work was by what? _____

What two things does God's **grace** do for us according to Ephesians 1:6-7?_____

_____

Ultimately, Ephesians 2:7-9 teaches us that God's **grace** is the key to what? _____

_____

Thank God for His **grace** and like Paul, pray that God's **grace** would be a major part of the lives of your friends and family.

5. **Amen**: The Greek/Hebrew word **amen** is translated **amen** 49 times and *verily* over 150 times in the New Testament. The word actually means *so be it* or *this is the truth*. Paul often ends his letters with this word meaning, "You can believe this because what I have written is the true, trustworthy words of God." I trust that in the last 6 weeks, everything we've learned together from this Bible study will impact and change our lives. May we live CHRIST-CENTERED lives in this SELF-CENTERED world. **Amen***?* **Amen**. **Amen***!*

> How did Paul's final words in Titus 3:15 touch your heart and motivate you to impact others by living a CHRIST-CENTERED (not a SELF-CENTERED) life? Amen?

SATURDAY REVIEW
Titus 3:9-11

How has God used Titus 3:9 to help you avoid foolish, time-wasting arguments so you can concentrate on living a CHRIST-CENTERED (not a SELF-CENTERED) life?

What did God teach you today from Titus 3:10-11 about dealing with SELF-CENTERED heretics who oppose a CHRIST-CENTERED life and ministry?

SUNDAY REVIEW
Titus 3:12-15

Titus lived a CHRIST-CENTERED life. What did you learn from Titus 3:12 that will help you to be like Titus, a guy people loved to have around?

How have the principles of Titus 3:13-14 encouraged you to be a CHRIST-CENTERED, fruitful believer who loves to do good, rather than a SELF-CENTERED, unfruitful believer who seldom does good?

How did Paul's final words in Titus 3:15 touch your heart and motivate you to impact others by living a CHRIST-CENTERED (not a SELF-CENTERED) life? Amen?

ENDNOTES

1 Dr. Bob Jones Sr., *Chapel Sayings of Dr. Bob Jones Sr.*, Bob Jones University, Greenville, South Carolina, p. 22.

2 John MacArthur, Jr., *MacArthur's New Testament Commentary: Titus*, The Moody Bible Institute of Chicago, Chicago, Illinois, 1996. (Electronic STEP Files, Parsons Technology, Inc., Hiawatha, Iowa, 1997.)

3 Albert Barnes, *Barnes Notes: The Gospels*, Baker Book House, Grand Rapids, Michigan, 1985, p. 159 and Albert Barnes, *Barnes Notes-Ephesians to Philemon*, Baker Book House, Grand Rapids, Michigan, 1985, pp. 114-115.

4 Warren Wiersbe, *The Bible Exposition Commentary: Volume 2*, Scripture Press Publications, Inc. (Division of Victor Books), Wheaton, Illinois, 1989, p. 263.

5 John Benton, Straightening Out the Self-Centered Church, The message of Titus, Welwyn Commentary Series, Evangelical Press, Darlington, Colorado, p. 143.

6 Warren Wiersbe, *The Bible Exposition Commentary: Volume 2*, Scripture Press Publications, Inc. (Division of Victor Books), Wheaton, Illinois, 1989, p. 267.

7 John MacArthur, Jr., *MacArthur's New Testament Commentary: Titus*, The Moody Bible Institute of Chicago, Chicago, Illinois, 1996. (Electronic STEP Files, Parsons Technology, Inc., Hiawatha, Iowa, 1997.)

8 Warren Wiersbe, *The Bible Exposition Commentary: Volume 2*, Scripture Press Publications, Inc. (Division of Victor Books), Wheaton, Illinois, 1989, p. 268.

CHRISTIAN ASSOCIATION, INC.

Since 1969, THE WILDS Christian Camp and Conference Center has been serving the local church with a wide variety of camping programs. Our summer season, with over 11,000 campers, focuses on juniors with our Junior Boot Camp, teens with our junior high/senior high camps, and families with our week-long Family Camps. Fall and spring bring an entirely different look to the mountains and a different array of camps including Couples' Retreats, school and church retreats, high school Senior Trips, Senior High Leadership Camps, Ladies' Retreats, Father/Son Campouts, Senior Adult Retreats, College and Career Retreats, and specialized conferences including a Music Conference, a Youth Workers' Conference, Deacons' Conferences, and a Pastors' Conference. During this non-summer season we annually serve more than 10,000 campers of all ages.

THE WILDS is located in the beautiful Blue Ridge Mountains of western North Carolina and is a stunning piece of God's handiwork. Blessed with four spectacular waterfalls, meandering streams, and miles of hiking trails on the property, the campsite shows forth the handiwork of God. In this beautiful setting, thousands of campers of every age have accepted Christ as Saviour and Lord and have surrendered to His will and to His service.

Natural outgrowths of this active camp ministry are a music publication ministry, offering the most refreshing of conservative Christian music, cantatas, CDs, a song and chorus book, piano books, and choral books for men, ladies, and mixed groups. As an outgrowth of the strong preaching and teaching ministries of the camp, THE WILDS has produced a great variety of Bible study helps, scripture memory programs, personal devotional helps, and books for individuals and group studies. In addition, CampsAbroad, the missions arm of THE WILDS, assists missionaries and nationals all over the world in the development and operation of Christian camp ministries. In 2009 THE WILDS of New England began ministry operations at our campsite in Deering, New Hampshire. In this peaceful, rural setting we anticipate a steady growth and planned development toward a year-round camp and conference ministry for this area of the country.

For more information about any of our camping programs, music publications, or other products from THE WILDS, please visit our website at www. wilds. org, or contact the administrative office:

THE WILDS Christian Association, Inc.
PO Box 509
Taylors, SC 29687-0009
Phone: (864) 268-4760 • Fax: (864) 292-0743
E-mail: info@wilds.org